W9-CFV-540

PIONEERS IN MATHEMATICS

THE BIRTH OF MATHEMATICS

Ancient Times to 1300

MICHAEL J. BRADLEY, PH.D.

CHELSEA HOUSE
PUBLISHERS
An imprint of Infobase Publishing

The Birth of Mathematics: Ancient Times to 1300

Chelsea House
An imprint of Infobase Publishing
132 West 31st Street
New York NY 10001

Library of Congress Cataloging-in-Publication Data

Bradley, Michael J.
    The birth of mathematics : ancient times to 1300 / Michael J. Bradley.
        p. cm.—(Pioneers in mathematics)
    Includes bibliographical references and index.
    ISBN 0-8160-5423-1 (acid-free paper)
    1. Mathematicians—Biography. 2. Mathematics, Ancient. 3. Mathematics—History—To 1300. I. Title.
    QA28.B73 2006
    510.9—dc22   2005030563

Text design by Mary Susan Ryan-Flynn
Cover design by Dorothy Preston
Illustrations by Dale Williams

Printed in the United States of America

MP FOF 10 9 8 7 6 5 4 3 2 1

This book is printed on acid-free paper.

CONTENTS

PREFACE

Mathematics is a human endeavor. Behind its numbers, equations, formulas, and theorems are the stories of the people who expanded the frontiers of humanity's mathematical knowledge. Some were child prodigies while others developed their aptitudes for mathematics later in life. They were rich and poor, male and female, well educated and self-taught. They worked as professors, clerks, farmers, engineers, astronomers, nurses, and philosophers. The diversity of their backgrounds testifies that mathematical talent is independent of nationality, ethnicity, religion, class, gender, or disability.

Pioneers in Mathematics is a five-volume set that profiles the lives of 50 individuals, each of whom played a role in the development and the advancement of mathematics. The overall profiles do not represent the 50 most notable mathematicians; rather, they are a collection of individuals whose life stories and significant contributions to mathematics will interest and inform middle school and high school students. Collectively, they represent the diverse talents of the millions of people, both anonymous and well known, who developed new techniques, discovered innovative ideas, and extended known mathematical theories while facing challenges and overcoming obstacles.

Each book in the set presents the lives and accomplishments of 10 mathematicians who lived during an historical period. *The Birth of Mathematics* profiles individuals from ancient Greece, India, Arabia, and medieval Italy who lived from 700 B.C.E. to 1300 C.E. *The Age of Genius* features mathematicians from Iran, France, England, Germany, Switzerland, and America who lived between the 14th and 18th centuries. *The Foundations of Mathematics* presents 19th-century mathematicians from various European countries. *Modern Mathematics* and *Mathematics Frontiers* profile a variety of international mathematicians who worked in the early 20th and the late 20th century, respectively.

The 50 chapters of Pioneers in Mathematics tell pieces of the story of humankind's attempt to understand the world in terms of numbers, patterns, and equations. Some of the individuals profiled contributed innovative ideas that gave birth to new branches of mathematics. Others solved problems that had puzzled mathematicians for centuries. Some wrote books that influenced the teaching of mathematics for hundreds of years. Still others were among the first of their race, gender, or nationality to achieve recognition for their mathematical accomplishments. Each one was an innovator who broke new ground and enabled their successors to progress even further.

From the introduction of the base-10 number system to the development of logarithms, calculus, and computers, most significant ideas in mathematics developed gradually, with countless individuals making important contributions. Many mathematical ideas developed independently in different civilizations separated by geography and time. Within the same civilization, the name of the scholar who developed a particular innovation often became lost as his idea was incorporated into the writings of a later mathematician. For these reasons, it is not always possible to identify accurately any one individual as the first person to have discovered a particular theorem or to have introduced a certain idea. But then mathematics was not created by one person or for one person; it is a human endeavor.

ACKNOWLEDGMENTS

An author does not write in isolation. I owe a debt of thanks to many people who helped in a myriad of ways during the creation of this work.

To Jim Tanton, who introduced me to this fascinating project.

To Jodie Rhodes, my agent, who put me in touch with Facts On File and handled the contractual paperwork.

To Frank K. Darmstadt, my editor, who kept me on track throughout the course of this project.

To Larry Gillooly, George Heffernan, and Ernie Montella, who assisted with the translations of Latin and Italian titles.

To Steve Scherwatzky, who helped me to become a better writer by critiquing early drafts of many chapters.

To Melissa Cullen-DuPont, who provided invaluable assistance with the artwork.

To Amy L. Conver, for her copyediting.

To my wife, Arleen, who provided constant love and support.

To the many relatives, colleagues, students, and friends who inquired and really cared about my progress on this project.

To Joyce Sullivan, Donna Katzman, and their students at Sacred Heart School in Lawrence, Massachusetts, who created poster presentations for a Math Fair based on some of these chapters.

To the faculty and administration of Merrimack College who created the Faculty Sabbatical Program and the Faculty Development Grant Program, both of which provided me with time to read and write.

INTRODUCTION

This first volume of the Pioneers in Mathematics set profiles the lives of 10 mathematicians who lived between 700 B.C.E. and 1300 C.E. During these 20 centuries, thousands of scholars from many civilizations introduced mathematical ideas that established the foundations of arithmetic, number theory, algebra, geometry, and trigonometry as well as the related sciences of astronomy and physics. All the great civilizations that flourished during these and earlier centuries developed mathematical innovations. We know very little about the specific individuals who made important discoveries and introduced new ideas in Babylonia, Egypt, and China. Historians in Greece, India, Arabia, and medieval Italy preserved a more complete record of their civilizations' mathematical discoveries and recorded the identities of some of the innovators. For this reason, this book profiles 10 individuals from these four cultures as representatives of the numerous scholars from all the cultures of this era.

During the first half of this 2,000-year period, Greek scholars developed a formalized system of practical and theoretical mathematics. In the seventh century B.C.E., Thales of Miletus helped to provide a logical basis for the discipline of mathematics by producing the earliest-known proofs of geometrical theorems. A century later, Pythagoras of Samos founded a school where he and his followers studied diverse mathematical ideas, including perfect numbers, the lengths of the sides of right triangles, and the five regular solids. In the third century B.C.E., Euclid of Alexandria wrote *Elements*, the book that defined the study of geometry for 2,000 years. His contemporary, Archimedes of Syracuse used innovative geometrical techniques to estimate perimeters, areas, and volumes, to determine tangent lines, and to trisect angles. In the fourth century c.e., Hypatia of Alexandria, the earliest-known woman to write and teach about higher mathematics, wrote commentaries that enhanced and preserved the works of earlier Greek scholars.

Generations of mathematicians in India also developed advanced ideas and techniques in various branches of mathematics. Two of the foremost Hindu scholars of this period were Āryabhata and Brahmagupta. In the sixth century, Āryabhata introduced an alphabetical system of notation to represent large numbers and developed techniques for estimating distances, determining areas, and calculating volumes. In the seventh century, Brahmagupta developed rules for performing arithmetic with negative numbers and introduced iterative algorithms to find sines of angles and square roots.

During the next six centuries, Arabic mathematicians further extended the discoveries of Greek and Indian scholars. The ninth-century mathematician Muhammad al-Khwārizmī demonstrated how to solve second-degree equations in the earliest-known text on algebra. In the 11th century, Omar Khayyám developed geometrical techniques for solving algebraic equations and expanded on Euclid's theory of ratios.

In 13th-century Italy, Leonardo Fibonacci wrote about the base-10 number system and the efficient computational algorithms that Hindu and Arabic scholars had developed. His book was one of several similar works on arithmetic and computation that caused western Europeans to renew their interest in Greek mathematics and convinced them to adopt the Hindu-Arabic numbering system.

These 10 mathematicians made additional significant contributions to the progress of mathematics and science. Thousands more of their colleagues and countrymen made important mathematical discoveries that advanced the world's knowledge. The stories of their achievements provide a glimpse into the lives and the minds of some of the pioneers who discovered mathematics.

Thales of Miletus

(ca. 625–ca. 547 B.C.E.)

Thales of Miletus proved the earliest theorems in geometry. *(The Granger Collection)*

Earliest Proofs of Geometrical Theorems

Thales (pronounced THAY-leez) of Miletus established the study of natural philosophy in a world dominated by Greek mythology. His proofs of five theorems in geometry introduced the concept of logical theory into mathematics. As an astronomer, he predicted a solar eclipse and improved the existing techniques for navigating by the stars. Thales became known throughout the ancient Greek

1

world for his ingenious solutions to practical problems involving pyramids, donkeys, rivers, and ships.

Early Years

Conflicting historical records place the date of Thales' birth between 641 and 625 B.C.E., although the later date is generally accepted as more accurate. He was born in Miletus, a small town located 200 miles east of Athens across the Aegean Sea in the Greek province of Ionia in present-day Turkey. Miletus was a seaport on the trade routes that linked the Mediterranean world with India and other countries of the Near East. As Thales traveled outside his local community, he became known as Thales of Miletus.

Little is known about Thales' family or his early life. Cleobuline and Examyes, his mother and father, respectively, were a distinguished family, but their careers and achievements are not known. As a young man, Thales traveled to Egypt and Babylonia (modern-day Iraq) to pursue his interests in astronomy, mathematics, and science. He learned how Egyptians used practical geometrical techniques to measure distances and to calculate areas of plots of farmland. He studied Babylonian astronomy and its use of a base-60 number system.

Natural Philosopher

Around 590 B.C.E., Thales returned to Miletus and established a school known as the Ionian School of Philosophy, where he taught science, astronomy, mathematics, and philosophy. In his philosophy classes, he shared with his students his ideas about the meaning of life and the love of wisdom. He stressed the importance of asking questions, especially the question "Why?" In all areas of study, he emphasized that the workings of the world could be explained in terms of logical, underlying theories.

At the time, Greeks believed that their lives were determined by the actions of many gods. According to their mythology, the god Demeter made crops and animals grow; the god Dionysus made wine taste sweet or bitter; the goddess Aphrodite made people fall in love; the god Ares decided who won wars. Thales did not accept stories about gods as explanations for why events occurred. He was convinced that there had to be natural reasons to explain why the world behaved as it did.

Like the people of his day, Thales believed the Earth was a large disk floating on an underground ocean of water. According to a Greek myth, the god Poseidon, who lived in this underground ocean, would shake the Earth, causing an earthquake when he was angry. Searching for a more logical and natural explanation, Thales reasoned that if waves in the sea could rock boats back and forth, then waves in this underground ocean could push against the ground from below, causing it to shake. He taught this theory to the students at his school and encouraged them to seek similar explanations for other physical occurrences.

Although Thales' theory about the cause of earthquakes was not correct, his search for natural rather than supernatural or mystical reasons to explain such events was a radically new approach to understanding the world. His insistence on natural explanations and unifying theories that linked a cause with its effect became known as natural philosophy. Aristotle, in his book *Metaphysics*, credited Thales as being the founder of Ionian natural philosophy. By searching for the laws of nature that explained physical phenomena, Thales paved the way for the development of science.

First Proofs of Theorems in Mathematics

In his school, Thales taught that mathematical ideas were logically connected to each other rather than being a collection of unrelated rules. He also believed that mathematical results were true not only because they agreed with our experiences of the world around us but also for deeper reasons. Thales searched for a set of basic principles and the logic that would allow him to develop all mathematical properties and rules from them. He called these basic principles axioms and postulates. A property that could be obtained from them by a logical argument was called a theorem, and the logical reasoning was called a proof.

Thales proved five theorems about geometrical properties of circles and triangles. These results were known to be true, but no one had explained *why* they were true. Thales showed how they followed logically from the basic axioms of geometry.

The following are the five theorems Thales proved:

1. Any line drawn through the center of a circle will divide that circle into two equal areas. In other words, any diameter bisects the circle.

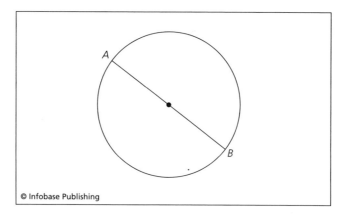

2. If a triangle has two sides that are equal in length, then the two angles opposite those sides must also be equal in measure. That is to say, the base angles of an isosceles triangle are equal.

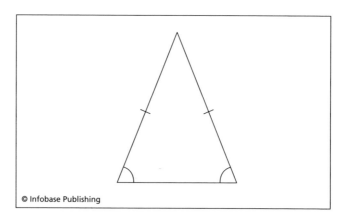

3. If two lines intersect, each pair of angles that open in opposite directions must be equal to each other. More efficiently stated, vertical angles formed by intersecting lines are equal.

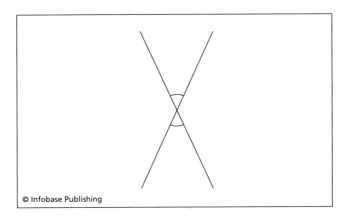

© Infobase Publishing

4. If the three vertices (the corner points) of a triangle are points on a circle, and if one of the three sides of the triangle is a diameter of the circle, then the triangle is a right triangle. In other words, a triangle inscribed in a semicircle must be a right triangle.

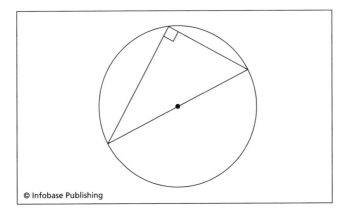

© Infobase Publishing

5. If two angles and the side between them in one triangle are the same measure as the two corresponding angles and the corresponding side of another triangle, then the two triangles are identical to each other. This is the "ASA rule" of congruent triangles.

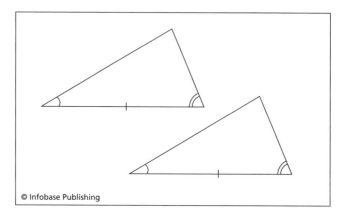

The original proofs that Thales gave for these first five mathematical theorems have been lost because he did not write any books on mathematics and because mathematicians in later years developed more elegant proofs of these results. Nevertheless, Thales' teaching that mathematical theorems must be proven redefined the nature of mathematics significantly. What had been a collection of techniques for measuring and rules for calculating was transformed into a powerful system of rational analysis. His emphasis on the use of logical reasoning from fundamental principles became essential to the study and practice of geometry and remains a basic characteristic of all branches of mathematics today.

Discoveries in Astronomy

In addition to being a philosopher and a mathematician, Thales was an accomplished astronomer. In 585 B.C.E., he correctly predicted an eclipse of the Sun. By studying records that Babylonian astronomers had kept for many years, Thales was able to determine when the Moon would pass in front of the Sun, blocking it from view in his part of the world. His ability to foretell this event and explain why it occurred amazed his Greek countrymen, who believed that the Sun's disappearance meant that the gods were mad at them. During his lifetime, he was better known for making this accurate prediction than for any of his other accomplishments.

Thales proposed theories to predict and explain the summer solstice—the longest day of the year—and the vernal and autumnal equinoxes—the days in the spring and fall when sunrise and sunset are 12 hours apart. Some historians claim that he wrote an astronomy book about eclipses, solstices, and equinoxes, but no copies of such a book have ever been found.

In addition to studying the Sun, Thales made observations of the stars. The Greeks had identified many groups of stars called constellations that seemed to be arranged as the outlines of the shapes of various animals and people. They gave them names such as Scorpio, Aquarius, Leo, and Gemini; named their months after 12 of these constellations; and developed an intricate theory called astrology that explained how a person's personality and fate were determined by the sign of the zodiac under which he or she was born. Thales did not believe in astrology but was interested in how the positions of the constellations could be used to help sailors determine their location and to guide them to their destinations while at sea. Greek sailors commonly used the constellation Ursa Major, also known as the Great Bear or Big Dipper, as one of their chief navigational guides. Thales identified a new constellation: Ursa Minor, also known as the Little Bear or the Little Dipper. This group of six stars—which included the North Star, one of the brightest stars in the sky—had a more reliable location in the sky. He recommended that sailors rely on this constellation to guide their travels. This recommendation appeared in a book on navigation titled *The Nautical Star Guide*. Although Thales probably developed the theory, scholars believe that the book was written by a contemporary named Phokos of Samos.

Ingenious Solutions to Practical Problems

Thales' reputation as a learned man became widespread. Wherever he traveled, people sought his advice to solve difficult problems. During a visit to Egypt, the Pharaoh asked Thales to determine the height of one of the pyramids. As he thought about how to approach this problem, Thales observed that the shadows of objects in the sun were different lengths at different times of the day. He reasoned that when his own shadow was as long as he was tall, then the pyramid's shadow would be as long as the pyramid was tall. By employing this simple principle, he determined the height of the pyramid successfully.

The Greek general Croesus sought Thales' advice to help his army cross the river Halys, which was too wide to build a bridge across and too deep to march through. After some thought, Thales instructed the general to bring all his men and their equipment near the riverbank. He then had them dig a canal behind them in the same direction that the river was flowing. When the ends of the

Thales determined the height of a pyramid by measuring the length of its shadow. *(Library of Congress, Prints and Photographs Division)*

canal were connected to the river, most of the water flowed from the river into the canal behind the army and back into the river further downstream. The army was then able to march through the shallow waters that remained.

Merchants and sailors who wanted an accurate way to determine how far a ship was from shore also brought their problem to Thales. Looking from the shore out to a ship that was leaving or entering their port, they could estimate how far away it was based on how small it appeared, but they wanted a more exact way to calculate the actual distance. Thales used his knowledge of similar triangles—triangles of different sizes that each have the same three angles—to develop a method for determining this distance precisely. He knew that for such a pair of triangles, the ratio of two sides of one triangle would be the same as the ratio of the corresponding sides of the other triangle.

The accompanying diagram illustrates Thales' technique. From two points on the shore (labeled A and B in the diagram), observe the location of the ship. Draw a new line through A that forms a

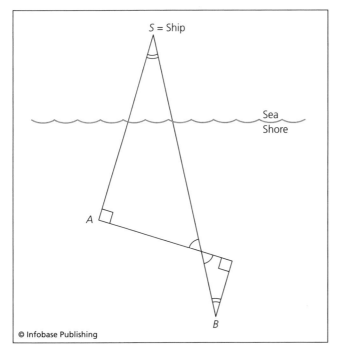

Thales developed a geometrical method to determine the distance from shore to a ship at sea.

right angle with this line of sight, then draw a line through *B* that forms a right angle with this new line. These lines and the lines of sight from points *A* and *B* to the ship will create two similar triangles. By measuring the four sides that are on the shore, one can use the ratios of the corresponding sides to calculate the distances to the ship. The merchants and sailors, who were very good at taking measurements and creating right angles, found this technique easy to use and very valuable.

Legends about Thales

Storytellers preserved and perhaps exaggerated Thales' greatness by creating legends about him, even though some of these stories may not have been true. The philosopher Aristotle told a story that showed how Thales' careful observations of the world allowed him to make a wise business deal. Olives were a very important crop in Greece. In addition to eating olives with most of their meals, Greeks also crushed them to collect olive oil that they used for cooking, as fuel for their lamps, and as an ointment for their skin. Thales had observed that, for several years, the weather had been unfavorable for growing olives. Reasoning that the bad weather could not last much longer, he visited olive orchards, offering to buy the equipment that had been used for crushing olives. The growers, who were in need of money, sold their olive presses to Thales. That year, the weather was excellent for growing olives. When the plentiful crops were harvested and it was time to make olive oil, Thales earned a lot of money renting out the olive presses to the same people who had just sold them to him. Soon afterward, Thales sold the presses back to the growers at fair prices, having demonstrated that he was not just a problem-solver; he could be a successful businessman as well.

Another story that was told about Thales involved a donkey that was used to carry bags of salt from a salt mine. According to this legend, the workers who dug the salt out of the mine would shovel it into sacks that they placed on the backs of donkeys. The animals carried their sacks of salt several miles to the seashore, where workers loaded the bags onto ships. Along the way, the donkeys had to cross a shallow river. One day while crossing the river, one of the donkeys stumbled and fell. As he lay in the river, most of his salt dissolved in the water. When he was able to get up, his load was much lighter, which made the remainder of the trip much easier for him. After that day, whenever he crossed the river, this donkey would fall in the water, lose some of his salt, and finish the trip with bags that weighed much less than they had originally. The men in charge of the mine asked doctors to examine the donkey to see if it had an injured leg. When no one could determine why the donkey kept stumbling in the river, they finally asked Thales for some help. After observing the donkey for a few days, Thales realized that it was intentionally falling in the water to lighten its load. The next day, Thales filled the donkey's bags with sponges instead of salt. This time, when the donkey fell while crossing the river, the sponges absorbed water, making its bags much heavier. After a few days of carrying wet sponges, the donkey was cured of its bad habit.

The Greek philosopher Plato told a story about Thales and his deep interest in observing the stars. According to this legend, when Thales was out looking up at the stars, he fell into a well. A young girl came by and found him in the well unable to climb out of the deep hole. When Thales told her who he was and what had happened, she laughed at him. She teased the wise man for being so intent on the distant stars above his head that he could not even see what was at his own feet. Plato told this story to make fun of impractical philosophers who were capable of great abstract thoughts but could not do simple things.

Other historians tell another story about Thales and a well that is more credible. In this story, he climbed down into the well to get a better view of the stars. From deep below ground, the walls of the well blocked out the light of the moon and other stars, allowing Thales to better see the stars in the portion of the sky that he wanted to study. In this story, Thales had a sensible reason for climbing down into the well.

Conclusion

Thales died at the age of 78 in approximately 547 B.C.E. During his lifetime, he established the study of natural philosophy, revolutionized the discipline of mathematics, and made contributions to the science of astronomy. His fame as a philosopher, mathematician, astronomer, and ingenious problem-solver was known throughout the entire Greek world. Storytellers made him the central figure in so many stories that his name became synonymous with the word *genius*, much as the name of Albert Einstein is today. His fellow countrymen honored his memory by naming him one of the Seven Wise Men of Ancient Greece—an indication of the respect and admiration that they had for this brilliant problem-solver.

Thales' primary influence on mathematics and science was to establish the need for a theoretical basis and the use of logical reasoning. His natural philosophy introduced the ideas that there are natural explanations for all physical phenomena and that various phenomena are unified by underlying principles. By proving the first theorems in geometry, Thales created a logical structure for the subject and introduced the concept of proof into mathematics. Without these ideas, there would be no modern scientific or mathematical theory; science and mathematics would continue to be a collection of practices that had been observed to work without an understanding of the theoretical principles that explained why things work the way they do.

FURTHER READING

Heath, Sir Thomas L. "Chapter 4. The Earliest Greek Geometry. Thales." In *A History of Greek Mathematics*. Vol. 1, *From Thales to Euclid*, 118–140. New York: Dover, 1981. An historical look at Thales' mathematical work.

Longrigg, James. "Thales." In *Dictionary of Scientific Biography*. Vol. 13, edited by Charles C. Gillispie, 295–298. New York: Scribner, 1972. Encyclopedic biography.

O'Connor, J. J., and E. F. Robertson. "Thales of Miletus." In "MacTutor History of Mathematics Archive." University of Saint Andrews. Available online. URL: http://turnbull.mcs.st-and.ac.uk/~history/Mathematicians/Thales.html. Accessed March 25, 2005. Online biography, from the University of Saint Andrews, Scotland.

Petechuk, David A. "Thales of Miletus." In *Notable Mathematicians from Ancient Times to the Present*, edited by Robin V. Young, 474–476. Detroit: Gale, 1998. Brief biographical sketch of Thales.

Reimer, Luetta and Wilbert Reimer. "Pyramids, Olive, and Donkeys: Thales." In *Mathematicians Are People, Too: Stories from the Lives of Great Mathematicians*, 1–7. Parsippany, N.J.: Seymour, 1990. Life story with historical facts and fictionalized dialogue; intended for elementary school students.

Turnbull, Herbert W. "Chapter 1. Early Beginnings: Thales, Pythagoras and the Pythagoreans." In *The Great Mathematicians*, 1–17. New York: New York University Press, 1961. An in-depth look at Thales' mathematical work.

2

Pythagoras of Samos

(ca. 560–ca. 480 B.C.E.)

Pythagoras of Samos made early discoveries in number theory and geometry. (*The Image Works*)

Ancient Greek Proves Theorem about Right Triangles

Pythagoras (pronounced pi-THAG-or-us) of Samos was a mathematician and religious leader in ancient Greece. Conducting some of the earliest work in number theory, he proved fundamental properties about groups of numbers that he termed *perfect*, *friendly*, *odd*, and *triangular*. Pythagoras discovered the mathematical ratios that form the basis of musical theory and proposed that the same ratios exist in astronomy. He gave the first proof of the

Pythagorean *theorem* about right triangles and, as a result, discovered irrational numbers. His work with the five regular solids illustrated the Greek culture's complicated blending of mysticism and mathematical theory.

First Student is Paid to Learn

Records from historians, mathematicians, and philosophers of the third, fourth, and fifth centuries B.C.E. provide contradictory dates that vary by more than 20 years for Pythagoras's birth, death, and the important events in his life. These sources indicate that Pythagoras was born between 584 and 560 B.C.E. on the island of Samos off the coast of Ionia (present-day Turkey). Although it lay 150 miles east of Athens in the Aegean Sea, Samos was a Greek colony at the time. During the Golden Age of Greece when Pythagoras lived, Samos was a prosperous seaport and cultural center of learning.

Details of Pythagoras's family life are sketchy. Mnesarchus, his father, was a traveling merchant; Pythais, his mother, raised Pythagoras and his two older brothers whose names are not known. At an early age, he showed a talent for arithmetic and music, two interests that he maintained throughout his entire life. Under the guidance of the Greek mathematician Thales, who lived in the nearby city of Miletus, Pythagoras studied mathematics and astronomy. At the age of 20, he traveled to Egypt and Babylonia (present-day Iraq), where he learned mathematics, astronomy, and philosophy—the study of the meaning of life.

Many legends have been told about Pythagoras, including the story of how he became a teacher. After returning to Samos without any teaching experience and lacking an established reputation as a scholar, Pythagoras was not able to attract any students. Desperate to teach, he offered to pay a young boy to become his first student. Each day he met with the boy on the street, taught him the day's lesson, and paid the boy his daily wage. When this arrangement exhausted Pythagoras's savings and he informed his student that their lessons would have to end, the boy offered to pay Pythagoras to continue teaching him.

Pythagorean Society Blends Mysticism with Mathematics

In 529 B.C.E., Pythagoras moved to Croton, a city in southern Italy, and established a school for adults known as the Pythagorean Society. He divided the men and women of his school into two groups. The *acoustici*, or "listeners," attended his lectures but could not ask questions; they learned solely by listening, observing, and thinking. After five years of studying religion and philosophy, successful listeners joined the advanced group of students. These *mathematici*, or "mathematicians," had obtained enough knowledge to ask questions and express their own opinions. They studied a wider variety of subjects, including astronomy, music, and mathematics. Through Pythagoras's emphasis on arithmetic and geometry, the word *mathematician* eventually came to mean one who studied numbers.

The Pythagoreans, as the members of the society were known, followed strict rules of behavior that reflected their founder's strong convictions. Since Pythagoras believed in reincarnation—the theory that, after people died, they were reborn as different animals—the Pythagoreans ate vegetarian diets, were kind to animals, and never wore wool or leather. They did not eat beans or touch white roosters because they regarded them as symbols of perfection. Valuing generosity and equality, the Pythagoreans shared their possessions and allowed women to participate as both students and teachers. The Pythagorean Society was given credit for all discoveries made by the members, and no written records were kept detailing the activities, teachings, or achievements of the group.

The motto "all is number" expressed Pythagoras's belief that numbers were the fundamental nature of being. He taught that each number had its own distinctive characteristics that determined the qualities and behavior of all things. One was not considered to be a number; it was the essence of all numbers. Two represented women and the differences of opinion. Three represented men and the harmony of agreement. Four, which could be visualized as a square having four equal angles and four equal sides, symbolized equality, justice, and fairness. Five, as the sum of three and two, signified marriage, the union of a man and a woman. As evidenced by expressions

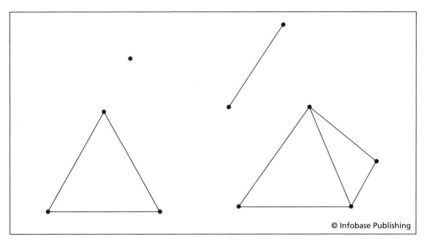

© Infobase Publishing

As evidence that "all is number," Pythagoras explained how points determine dimensions.

such as "fair and square" and "a square deal," these Pythagorean ideas became a regular part of Greek language and culture.

Numbers having distinctive mathematical properties fascinated Pythagoras. He called 7 a magical number because it was the only number between 2 and 10 that could not be obtained by multiplying or dividing two of the other numbers. Equations such as $2 \times 5 = 10$; $3 \times 3 = 9$; $8 \div 4 = 2$; and $6 \div 2 = 3$ produced all the numbers in this range except 7. He discovered that 16 was the only number that could be both the area and the perimeter of the same square, a square with all sides of length 4, and that 18 was the only number that could be the area and the perimeter of the same rectangle, a 3×6 rectangle. Pythagoras considered 10 to be holy because it was the sum of 1, 2, 3, and 4, the numbers that defined all the dimensions in the physical world: 1 point represented zero dimensions, 2 points determined a one-dimensional line, 3 points specified a two-dimensional triangle, and 4 points defined a three-dimensional pyramid.

Early Research in Number Theory

Pythagoras's investigations of numbers extended beyond numerology—the mixture of arithmetic, mysticism, and magic—to the

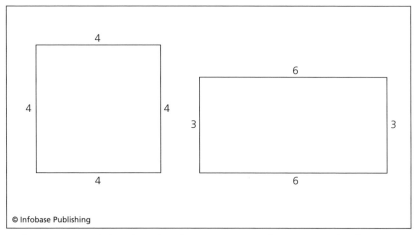

© Infobase Publishing

Pythagoras proved that there is only one square and one rectangle whose areas are equal to their perimeters.

branch of mathematics known as number theory. He identified many different groups of numbers based on the arithmetic properties they possessed, such as the concepts of even and odd numbers. A number was even if it could be separated into two equal parts; otherwise it was odd. He further subdivided the even numbers into the even-odds that could be written as two times an odd number (such as $6 = 2 \times 3$), the odd-evens that could be written as more than one factor of two times an odd number (such as $12 = 2 \times 2 \times 3$), and the even-evens that only had factors of two (such as $8 = 2 \times 2 \times 2$).

Pythagoras categorized numbers that could be arranged into similar geometric shapes. He called 3, 6, and 10 triangular numbers and 4, 9, and 16 square numbers because these quantities of dots could be configured into triangular and square patterns. Oblong numbers such as 6, 12, and 20 could be arranged as rectangles with one side being one unit longer than the other. He also studied numbers that could be organized into pentagons (five-sided figures), hexagons (six-sided figures), and other patterns. In addition to identifying various classes of numbers, Pythagoras and his students studied properties of these classes of numbers. They proved that every square number could be written as the sum of two triangular numbers, that every oblong number was twice a triangular number, and many other relationships.

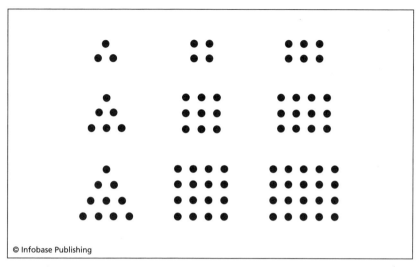

Triangular, square, and oblong numbers take their names from the geometrical shapes that they form.

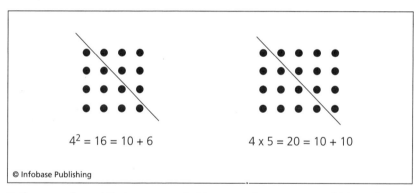

$4^2 = 16 = 10 + 6$ $4 \times 5 = 20 = 10 + 10$

Pythagoras showed that square and oblong numbers are sums of triangular numbers.

How a number compared to the sum of its factors—those smaller numbers that divided it—determined three more categories of numbers that Pythagoras called perfect, over-perfect, and deficient. A number such as 6 that was equal to the sum of its factors was perfect; 6 could only be divided by 1, 2, or 3 and was equal to 1 + 2 + 3. An over-perfect (or abundant) number such as 12 was divisible by too many numbers; its factors 1, 2, 3, 4, and 6 added up to more than 12. A deficient number such as 15 did not have enough divisors; its

Numbers that divide 220	Numbers that divide 284
1, 2, 4, 5, 10, 11, 20, 22, 44, 55, 110 sum = 284	1, 2, 4, 71, 142 sum = 220

© Infobase Publishing

The divisors of 220 add up to 284, and the divisors of 284 add up to 220.

factors 1, 3, and 5 added up to less than 15. Through his investigations, Pythagoras discovered only four perfect numbers: 6, 28, 496, and 8128. Friendly (or amicable) numbers—two numbers each equal to the sum of the other's factors—were even rarer. The numbers 220 and 284 were the only friendly pair that he was able to identify.

Pythagoras's work with these categories of numbers was the first systematic research in number theory. Modern number theorists continue to study the classes of numbers that he identified. Their work has important applications, including decoding messages and sending files securely over the Internet.

Ratios in Music and Astronomy

In addition to studying whole numbers, Pythagoras studied fractions. He believed that any measurement could be expressed as a whole number or as a fraction (also called a ratio) of two whole numbers. This idea of commensurability formed a basic assumption for his theory that "all is number."

Pythagoras discovered that ratios of whole numbers formed the foundations of musical harmony. As he studied the construction of musical instruments such as the lyre, a stringed instrument like a harp, he noticed that the most pleasing harmonies were produced by plucking strings whose lengths were in simple ratios. A string that was half as long as another produced the same tone but one octave higher. Strings that were $\frac{2}{3}$ and $\frac{3}{4}$ as long as each other produced pleasant-sounding chords called fifths and fourths. He identified the ratios that determined all the notes of the A-B-C-D-E-F-G musical scale.

From his observations of the motions of the planets, the Sun, the Moon, and the stars, Pythagoras developed an innovative astronomical theory based on this same pattern of ratios. According to his theory, the universe was a sphere with the stars moving on its outer shell and the Earth sitting at its center. The planets, Sun, and Moon rotated in circular orbits around the Earth. Pythagoras recorded how long it took each body to complete its orbit and determined the radius of each orbit. According to his computations, the distances from the Earth to each of the seven heavenly bodies—the Moon, Mercury, Venus, the Sun, Mars, Jupiter, and Saturn—generated the same ratios as the seven musical notes A through G. He concluded that as the planets moved through the universe they created a natural musical harmony that he called the "Harmony of the Spheres" or the "Music of the Spheres."

Pythagoras's discovery of the mathematical ratios of musical notes remains a fundamental result in the theory of musical acoustics. Although his theory of the Harmony of the Spheres gained widespread acceptance throughout the Greek world, scientists later disproved it. Some of his other work in astronomy, however, was accurate. By observing the curved shadow that the Earth cast on the Moon during a lunar eclipse, he determined that the Earth was a sphere. He also theorized correctly that the Earth rotated on its axis and that the Morning Star and the Evening Star were the same heavenly body.

Pythagorean Theorem

During his travels to Egypt and Babylonia, Pythagoras had learned the well-known property of triangles that if the lengths of the sides of a triangle were 3, 4, and 5, then the triangle had to be a right triangle. The lengths 3, 4, and 5 were related by the equation $3^2 + 4^2 = 5^2$, or $9 + 16 = 25$. The Egyptians were familiar with the principle that, if the sides of a triangle were of lengths a, b, and c and they satisfied the equation $a^2 + b^2 = c^2$, then the triangle had to be a right triangle. They also recognized that every right triangle had to satisfy this equation. Although they had not logically proven these mathematical truths, they accepted them and used them to design buildings, lay out farmland, and plan roadways based on right angles. The Babylonians had also discovered that, for any odd number n, the lengths n, $\dfrac{(n^2-1)}{2}$ and $\dfrac{(n^2+1)}{2}$ would form the three sides of a right triangle. Using these formulas, they were able to create an unlimited number of right triangles whose sides were whole numbers such as 3-4-5, 5-12-13, and 7-24-25 triangles.

Pythagoras created the first proof that in every right triangle, the lengths of the sides are related by the equation $a^2 + b^2 = c^2$. This property of right triangles has come to be known as the Pythagorean theorem, and a set of three numbers that satisfies this equation, such as 3-4-5, 8-15-17, or 20-21-29, are called a Pythagorean triple. The Pythagorean theorem is one of the most important results in mathematics. It is used in algebra, where it is the basis for calculating the distance between two points; in analytic geometry, where it

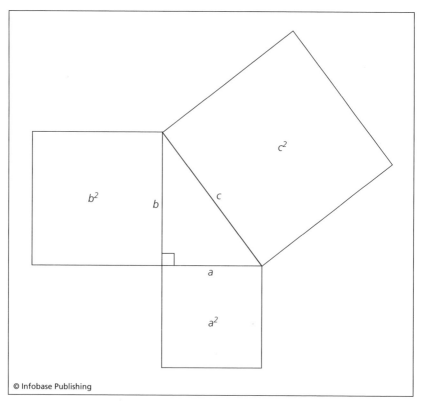

The Pythagorean theorem states that the sides of every right triangle are related by the equation $a^2 + b^2 = c^2$.

provides the equations of circles, ellipses, and parabolas; in trigo-nometry, where it describes a fundamental property of sines and cosines; and in many other branches of mathematics. The diagram that Pythagoras used in his proof of the theorem—a right triangle with a square attached to each of the three sides—remains one of the most recognizable images in mathematics.

Irrational Numbers

Pythagoras's work on this theorem led him to the controversial discovery that some numerical quantities could not be expressed as whole numbers or their ratios. He noticed that the diagonal of a square, the line joining two opposite corners, cut the square into two right triangles. If the sides of the square were each one unit long and the diagonal was x units long, then the sides of each right triangle satisfied the equation $1^2 + 1^2 = x^2$, or, more simply, $2 = x^2$.

To estimate the value of this diagonal length x, Pythagoras devised a method of calculating the ratios of the pairs of numbers listed in the following chart. The chart's first row contained the numbers 1 and 1. In each subsequent row, the first number was found by adding the two numbers in the previous row; the second number was found by adding the first number in that row to the first number in the previous row.

Pythagoras discovered that the ratios of these pairs of numbers—$\frac{1}{1}, \frac{3}{2}, \frac{7}{5}, \frac{17}{12}$, etc.—provided better estimates for the length of the

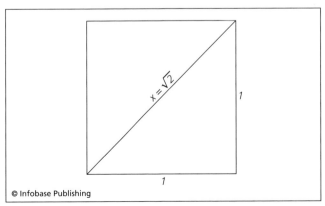

© Infobase Publishing

The sides and the diagonal of a square are related by the Pythagorean theorem.

A	B	Ratio of B/A	Decimal value of B/A
1	1	1/1	1.00000
2	3	3/2	1.50000
5	7	7/5	1.40000
12	17	17/12	1.41667
29	41	41/29	1.41379
70	99	99/70	1.41429
169	239	239/169	1.41420

© Infobase Publishing

Pythagoras used this chart of integer ratios to estimate the value of $\sqrt{2}$.

diagonal but that this sequence of fractions continued forever without becoming equal to the diagonal length. He ultimately proved that this length, $x = \sqrt{2}$, called the square root of 2, could not be written as a fraction. Working with more and more triangles, Pythagoras and his students found many other lengths, such as $\sqrt{3}$, $\sqrt{5}$, and $\sqrt{6}$, that could not be written as fractions.

The discovery of these irrational numbers (or incommensurables) contradicted Pythagoras's belief that everything in the universe could be expressed in terms of whole numbers and fractions. At first he required that the members of the Pythagorean Society swear an oath not to reveal this discovery to anyone outside the school. According to one legend, when a student named Hippasus broke this code of silence, he drowned mysteriously at sea. In time, Pythagoras reluctantly accepted the existence of irrationals and eventually incorporated them into his further research.

Irrational numbers were a key feature in the five-pointed star, or pentagram, that became the symbol of the Pythagorean Society. Members sewed this geometric design onto their clothing or drew it on the palms of their hands so they could recognize each other. Each point of intersection of two sides of the pentagram cut the sides into lengths that formed a ratio known as the golden mean or golden section. In the diagram below, point B cuts segment AC into lengths that satisfy the equation $\dfrac{AC}{AB} = \dfrac{AB}{BC}$. Both fractions in this

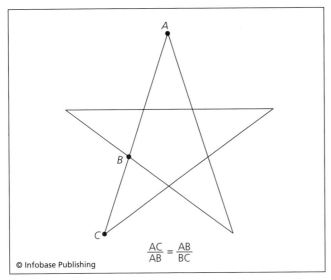

© Infobase Publishing

$$\frac{AC}{AB} = \frac{AB}{BC}$$

The Pythagoreans adopted the five-sided star known as the pentagram as their official symbol.

equation are equal to the golden mean, a value of $\frac{1+\sqrt{5}}{2}$, or approximately 1.618. Pythagoras and generations of Greek architects and sculptors considered this ratio to be the most beautiful of all proportions. They used it in their designs of many sculptures and buildings; most prominently, in the Parthenon in Athens.

Five Regular Solids

Pythagoras's work with regular solids was another important advance in geometry. A regular polygon, such as an equilateral triangle, a square, or a five-sided pentagon, is a two-dimensional figure in which all the edges have the same length. A regular solid (or polyhedron) is a three-dimensional object in which every side (or face) is the same regular polygon. At the time of Pythagoras, mathematicians knew only three regular solids—a triangular pyramid (or tetrahedron) that combined four equilateral triangles of the same size, a cube that could be made from six equal-sized squares, and a dodecahedron that was constructed

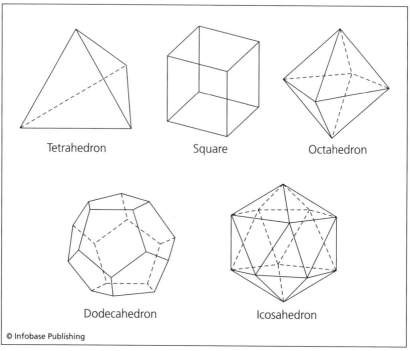

Tetrahedron   Square   Octahedron

Dodecahedron   Icosahedron

Pythagoras proved that there are only five regular solids.

from 12 regular pentagons. Pythagoras discovered how to make two additional regular solids. He showed that eight equilateral triangles could be combined to create a shape that he called an octahedron and that 20 equilateral triangles could form an object that he called an icosahedron. In addition to discovering these two new polyhedra, he proved that there were no other regular solids. His sophisticated argument, based on a thorough understanding of the geometry of two- and three-dimensional objects, demonstrated how advanced he had become in both mathematical knowledge and logical reasoning.

Although Pythagoras developed the complete theory of regular polyhedra, these five regular solids were eventually named after the great Greek philosopher Plato, who wrote about them 150 years later in his book *Timaeus*. Plato taught that the tetrahedron, the cube, the octahedron, and the icosahedron were the shapes of the atoms of the four elements from which the world was made—fire, earth, air, and water—and that the dodecahedron was the shape of the universe. In the 900 years that people studied at Plato's Academy, his teachings about these objects were so influential that the five regular solids became known as the Platonic solids.

Around 500 B.C.E., an angry mob burned down the Pythagoreans' school. According to one legend, Pythagoras died in the fire. According to another story, he escaped the fire but was chased by a mob to the edge of a bean field. Not wanting to step on the sacred bean plants, he stopped and was killed by the angry crowd. Other historians reported that he escaped the fire and lived the last years of his life in the nearby city of Metapontum, where he died in 480 B.C.E. After Pythagoras died, his followers started new schools in several other cities, where they carried on his traditions for two centuries.

Conclusion

After their leader's death, the members of the Pythagorean Society made many additional discoveries in mathematics. In algebra, they developed methods for solving more than one equation at the same time. They continued Pythagoras's work in number theory, discovering many properties of prime numbers. The Pythagoreans developed a theory of proportions that expanded the concept of the golden mean. In geometry, they determined how to calculate the sum of the angles in any polygon as well as the sum of the angles outside the polygon. They developed the method of application of areas to construct a square having the same area as a given triangle and introduced the words *parabola*, *hyperbola*, and *ellipse* in the process.

Twenty-four centuries after Pythagoras died, the Mathematical Association of America, one of the professional organizations of college math professors in the United States, chose the icosahedron as its official symbol. This figure that he discovered appears at the top of their stationery and on the covers of all their mathematical journals. Researchers in number theory continue to investigate many concepts that Pythagoras pioneered, including odd and even numbers; triangular, square, and oblong numbers; perfect, over-perfect, and deficient numbers; friendly numbers; and prime numbers. The Pythagorean theorem, irrational numbers, and Platonic solids are tools that modern mathematicians and scientists continue to use in their research.

FURTHER READING

Heath, Sir Thomas L. "Chapter 5. Pythagorean Geometry." In *A History of Greek Mathematics*. Vol. 1, *From Thales to Euclid*, 141–169. New York: Dover, 1981. A historical look at Pythagoras's mathematical work.

O'Connor, J. J., and E. F. Robertson. "Pythagoras of Samos." In "MacTutor History of Mathematics Archive." University of Saint Andrews. Available online. URL: http://turnbull.mcs.st-and.ac.uk/~history/Mathematicians/Pythagoras.html. Accessed March 25, 2005. Online biography, from the University of Saint Andrews, Scotland.

Petechuk, David A. "Pythagoras of Samos." In *Notable Mathematicians from Ancient Times to the Present*, edited by Robin V. Young, 407–408. Detroit: Gale, 1998. Brief biography.

Reimer, Luetta, and Wilbert Reimer. "The Teacher Who Paid His Student: Pythagoras." In *Mathematicians Are People, Too: Stories from the Lives of Great Mathematicians*, 8–17. Parsippany, N.J.: Seymour, 1990. Life story with historical facts and fictionalized dialogue; intended for elementary school students.

Turnbull, Herbert W. "Chapter 1. Early Beginnings: Thales, Pythagoras and the Pythagoreans." In *The Great Mathematicians*, 1–17. New York: New York University Press, 1961. An in-depth look at Pythagoras's mathematical work.

von Fritz, Kurt. "Pythagoras of Samos." In *Dictionary of Scientific Biography*. Vol. 11, edited by Charles C. Gillispie, 219–225. New York: Scribner, 1972. Encyclopedic biography.

3

Euclid of Alexandria

(ca. 325–ca. 270 B.C.E.)

Euclid of Alexandria formulated the principles and techniques that characterized the study of geometry for 2,000 years. *(The Granger Collection)*

Geometer Who Organized Mathematics

The ideas developed by Euclid (pronounced YEW-klid) of Alexandria defined the study of geometry for 2,000 years. *Elements*, his book on geometry and number theory, became the model for the logical development of mathematical theories from first principles and remains the most popular math book ever written. Euclid proved that there are infinitely many prime numbers and developed the Euclidean algorithm for finding the greatest common divisor of two numbers. Attempts to prove his parallel postulate led to the controversial discovery of non-Euclidean geometries in the 19th century. His writings dominated the study of geometry for so many centuries that people simply referred to him as "The Geometer."

Professor of Mathematics

Although he was born of Greek parents, lived in the Greek world, and wrote and taught in the Greek language, the details of Euclid's life are best known from the writings of Arab scholars who lived hundreds of years later. According to these sources, Euclid was born around 325 B.C.E. in Tyre, a large city at the eastern end of the Mediterranean Sea in present-day Lebanon. His father's name was Naucrates, and his grandfather's name was Zenarchus. After living for a number of years in the city of Damascus in present-day Syria, he moved to Athens, the capital of Greece.

Euclid became a student at the distinguished school that had been established in 387 B.C.E. by the Greek philosopher Plato. Since it was located in the town named Academy just outside Athens, this small but excellent university became known as Plato's Academy. For 900 years, people came from all parts of Greece and from many other countries to learn science, mathematics, and philosophy—the study of the meaning of life—in the tradition of this famous teacher. Plato placed such a high value on the study of mathematics that, according to one legend, he hung a sign over the front door of the academy that read "Let no one ignorant of mathematics enter here." All students at the academy learned advanced mathematics, and most of the accomplished mathematicians of the era studied at this school.

Around 300 B.C.E., Euclid moved to Alexandria, Egypt, where he spent the rest of his life. Because he earned his reputation for the work that he did while living there, he became known as Euclid of Alexandria. This large city at the mouth of the Nile River was the intellectual and commercial center of the Mediterranean world. The warrior-king Alexander the Great established Alexandria in 332 B.C.E. after he conquered the kingdom of Egypt. He and his successor Ptolemy built a massive library where they hoped to collect every book in existence. Whenever learned people came to Alexandria, their books were brought to the library, where scribes made handwritten copies of them. In this manner, the library amassed an extensive collection of more than half-a-million books.

In this city of culture and diversity, Ptolemy also established an institution for research and scholarly activities known as the Museum of Alexandria. This university, which was much larger than Plato's Academy, attracted the greatest minds from every country to discuss, learn, teach, and discover new ideas. Euclid became the first mathematics professor at the museum, where he earned a reputation as a kind and patient teacher. At the museum, he assembled a large group of mathematicians who built a strong reputation for doing research and for discovering new mathematical ideas. Generations of scholars continued this tradition, making the Museum of Alexandria a vibrant research community for 600 years.

Elements

Euclid's greatest achievement was *Elements*, a work in which he organized and presented all the elementary mathematics known at the time. Although Euclid called each of the 13 volumes a "book," they were more like the chapters of a single book. He wrote six chapters on plane geometry, four chapters dealing with properties of numbers, and three chapters on solid geometry. Each chapter included a sequence of propositions and problems. The 465 propositions presented the rules of mathematics stating what conclusions could be drawn from given sets of assumptions. Each proposition was followed by a logical argument called a proof that explained why the proposition was true. Worked-out examples called problems illustrated how to use the propositions in particular situations.

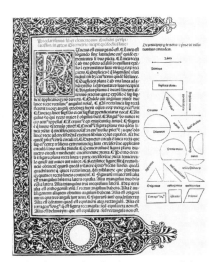

In his famous book *Elements*, Euclid logically developed the theorems of geometry and number theory from basic terms, postulates, and axioms. *(Library of Congress, Prints and Photographs Division)*

In this book, Euclid started from a simple foundation—23 basic terms, five postulates, and five axioms—and developed systematically all the known elementary mathematics of his day. The basic terms were fundamental ideas such as *point*, *line*, and *circle*. Postulates were basic concepts for geometry, such as the idea that through any two points there could be only one line. Axioms, or common notions, were ideas that were fundamental to all mathematics, such as things that are equal to the same thing are equal to each other. Where clear and accurate proofs of propositions existed, Euclid included them. Where known arguments could be improved, he substituted better ones. He organized the material into a meaningful sequence so that each chapter was a coherent unit and the 13 chapters comprised a complete collection.

The fist six books of *Elements* presented the rules and techniques of plane geometry. Book I included theorems about congruent triangles, constructions using a ruler and compass, and the proof of the Pythagorean theorem about the lengths of the sides of a right triangle. Book II presented geometric versions of the distributive law $a(b + c + d) = ab + ac + ad$ and formulas about squares, such as $(a + b)^2 = a^2 + 2ab + b^2$ and $a^2 - b^2 = (a + b)(a - b)$. Books III and IV covered the geometry of circles, including results about tangent and secant lines as well as the construction of inscribed and circumscribed polygons. The last two books on plane geometry introduced the theory of proportions and used these results to construct triangles and parallelograms whose sides and areas satisfied specified requirements.

The next four books, or chapters—VII, VIII, IX, and X—presented a collection of ideas in number theory. The first of these books discussed ratios, factors, and least-common multiples of whole numbers always representing each number as a line segment. Book VIII presented results about geometric sequences; plane numbers that have two factors, such as $10 = 5 \cdot 2$; and solid numbers that have three factors, such as $42 = 2 \cdot 3 \cdot 7$. The theorems in Book IX provided results about odd, even, perfect, and prime numbers. Book X, the longest in the work, presented 115 propositions on incommensurable or irrational numbers from a geometric point of view.

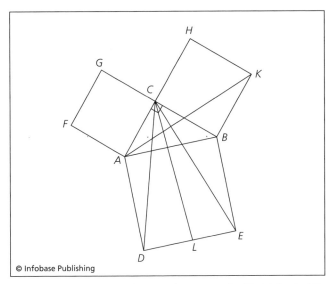

© Infobase Publishing

Euclid used the famous diagram known as the "bride's chair" to prove the Pythagorean theorem in Book I of *Elements*.

The final three books of *Elements* discussed three-dimensional geometry. Book XI presented procedures for constructing a line through a point that is perpendicular to a plane and for reproducing a boxlike figure known as a parallelepiped. Book XII provided techniques for calculating the volumes of pyramids, cones, cylinders, and spheres. The final book discussed properties of the five regular solids.

Original Results in *Elements*

Most of the material in *Elements* was not original. Euclid built on earlier mathematics texts, also called *Elements*, written in the fourth and fifth centuries B.C.E. by Hippocrates of Chios, Leon, and Theudius. He included the theorems Thales proved about angles, triangles, and circles. The material on proportions came from the work of Eudoxus. The first two chapters on plane geometry, many of the results from number theory, and most of the final chapter on the construction of the five regular solids were primarily the work of Pythagoras.

Mathematicians believe that at least two of the important propositions presented in Euclid's *Elements* were his own discoveries. Proposition 1 in Book VII introduced a technique now called the Euclidean algorithm for determining the greatest common divisor of a pair of numbers, the largest number that divides both of them without leaving a remainder. Using this algorithm, one can find the greatest common divisor of 240 and 55 by making the following sequence of calculations:

$240 \div 55$ leaves a remainder of 20.

$55 \div 20$ leaves a remainder of 15.

$20 \div 15$ leaves a remainder of 5.

$15 \div 5$ leaves no remainder.

Therefore, the greatest common divisor of 240 and 55 is 5. This simple process, one of the oldest-known techniques in number theory, is still presented as an important method of solution in modern textbooks on the subject.

Proposition 20 in Book IX gave Euclid's ingenious proof that there were infinitely many prime numbers—whole numbers like 2, 3, 5, and 7 that cannot be divided by any numbers other than themselves and one. In this proof, he reasoned that if there were only finitely many primes, multiplying them all together and adding 1 would produce a number that either was a new prime or could be divided by some new prime. Since both cases contradicted the original assumption that there were finitely many primes, he concluded that there must be infinitely many primes. Euclid's proof by contradiction was a masterpiece of logic, a classic result that is taught in modern college-level courses in mathematical logic.

Although other mathematicians had written books similar to *Elements*, none of them had the same impact as Euclid's work. His book set a new standard for mathematical reasoning and explanation. All later mathematical writers embraced his use of logical proofs based on first principles. His ideas on geometry so dominated that branch of mathematics that for centuries mathematicians referred to him as "The Geometer." In the past 2,300 years, more than 1,000 editions of *Elements* have been published in dozens of languages. When the printing press was invented in the 15th century, it was the first math book to be printed. More copies of Euclid's *Elements* have been printed than any other book except the Bible, and more students have used this book than any other textbook on any subject.

Criticisms of Euclid's Methods

Euclid understood that mathematics was useful for solving practical problems such as building bridges, designing efficient machines, and operating successful businesses, but he believed that the real value of mathematics was that it developed a person's mind. Studying mathematics enabled a person to become a disciplined thinker, to make logical arguments, and to appreciate abstract concepts. Mathematics searched for truths that existed outside of the human mind; it was not colored by emotions or opinions. For these reasons, he thought every intelligent person would benefit from a thorough study of mathematics.

His students did not always share Euclid's enthusiasm for the beauty and value of mathematics. According to a popular legend, when a discouraged student asked what he would get from learning mathematics, Euclid told one of his slaves to give the young man a coin so that he could make a profit from his studies. According to another legend, when the emperor Ptolemy attended Euclid's lectures on geometry, he became frustrated by Euclid's thorough and rigorous progression through the material. Accustomed to having clothing, furniture, a chariot, and even royal roads for his exclusive use, Ptolemy asked if there was an easier way to learn the subject. Euclid replied, "There is no royal road to geometry."

Even other mathematicians criticized Euclid for including in *Elements* the proofs of properties that were clearly true. They argued that it was obvious to anyone, even to a donkey, that the sum of the lengths of any two sides of a triangle had to be greater than the third side. Euclid explained that he proved this principle from other postulates and propositions rather than accepting it as an assumption in order to develop all of elementary mathematics logically from as few basic statements as possible.

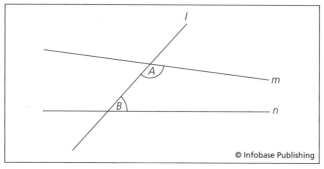

Euclid's controversial fifth postulate states that lines *m* and *n* must meet if angles *A* and *B* are less than 180°.

Parallel Postulate

The first four postulates in *Elements* were simple ideas, but the fifth postulate was more complicated. This statement about the angles formed by three intersecting lines meant that, given a point and a line, there was only one line that could be drawn through the point that did not eventually meet the other line. Two such lines that did not meet (or intersect) were said to be parallel. Mathematicians tried unsuccessfully to show that this parallel postulate was really a proposition by attempting to prove that it followed logically from the other postulates. The system of geometry that included Euclid's five postulates became known as Euclidean geometry. In the 19th century, several young mathematicians proved that the parallel postulate was an independent assumption that could not be proven from the other postulates. Substituting different postulates about parallel lines, they created mathematical systems called non-Euclidean geometries.

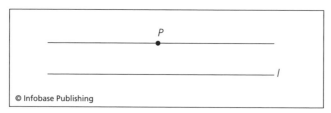

In Euclid's geometry, there is only one line through point *P* that does not meet line *l*.

In 1854, German mathematician Georg Riemann developed a theory about geometry on the surface of a sphere. In this geometry, he defined lines to be the "great circles" that passed through two points on the opposite ends of a sphere. On the surface of a globe, the lines of longitude that pass through the North and South Poles are examples of great circles. In this geometry, there were no parallel lines; any two lines would have to meet in two points. As a consequence, the angles in any triangle added up to more than 180°, rather than exactly 180° as in Euclidean geometry.

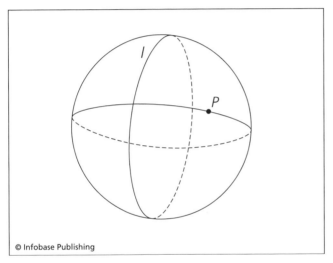

© Infobase Publishing

In Riemann's geometry, every line through point *P* must meet line *l*.

In 1826, Russian mathematician Nicholas Lobachevsky developed a different non-Euclidean geometry on a pseudosphere—a surface that looked like two trumpet horns glued together. In this geometrical system, there were infinitely many lines passing through a given point that did not intersect a given line. It followed logically that in every triangle, the three angles added up to less than 180°. Hungarian Janos Bolyai in 1823 and German Carl Friedrich Gauss in 1824 also discovered the existence of hyperbolic geometries with infinitely many parallel lines and triangles whose angles summed to less than 180°.

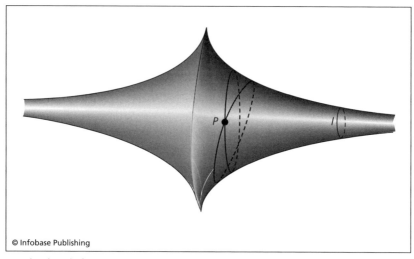

© Infobase Publishing

In Lobachevsky's geometry, there are infinitely many lines through point *P* that do not meet line *l*.

Initially, the mathematical community reacted negatively to the discoveries of these non-Euclidean geometries and criticized the mathematicians who discovered them. Eventually, mathematicians realized that non-Euclidean systems were legitimate, that they did not diminish Euclid's work, and that they had practical applications in physics and other sciences.

Euclid's Additional Writings

In addition to writing *Elements*, Euclid also wrote 15 other books on various topics in mathematics and science. His plane geometry text *Data* gave a compilation of facts involving proportions, triangles, circles, parallelograms, and other figures. This work, which may have been a companion book to *Elements*, presented the conclusions that could be drawn from knowing the lengths, areas, or proportions of the various geometrical components in 95 different situations. *On Divisions of Figures* explained how to cut circles, rectangles, and triangles into smaller pieces having particular sizes and shapes. Its 36 propositions showed how to draw a line that cut a triangle into a trapezoid and a triangle having equal areas, how to draw two parallel lines that cut off a desired fraction of a circle, and how to create a rectangle whose

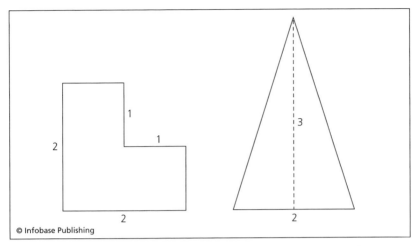

Euclid's *On Divisions of Figures* explained how to create geometrical figures having specified areas and edge lengths. The area and the base of this triangle are equal to the area and the base of a 2 × 2 square from which a smaller 1 × 1 square has been removed.

area was the same as another rectangle from which a square had been removed. The solutions of these types of geometrical puzzles required a deep understanding of the principles of plane geometry.

Two of Euclid's physics books provided the mathematical basis for scientific theories from optics and astronomy. In *Optics*, he discussed the laws of perspective and explained the process of vision. He presented the commonly accepted theory that a person's eye sent out rays that traveled in straight lines toward an object being viewed. Although this theory is incorrect because the human eye receives light rays that are emitted from a light source or are reflected by an object, his mathematical explanations accurately described many other aspects of the process of vision. He explained why objects of different sizes appeared to be the same size when they were viewed at certain angles and why parallel lines appeared to meet. In *Phenomena*, he presented a collection of theorems from spherical geometry and used them to present the geometrical basis for the motion of the stars and planets through the sky. He borrowed much of the material for this book from a similar work called *Sphaerica* (On spheres), written a few years earlier by the Greek mathematician Autolycus of Pitane.

Euclid wrote 11 other books that did not survive and are known only because they were mentioned in the writings of later authors. *Conics* was a four-volume work in which Euclid collected and rearranged all the known theories about the parabolic, elliptical, and hyperbolic curves that arise from slicing a cone-shaped object. Euclid drew most of the material in this work from an earlier work, *Solid Loci*, written by his contemporary Aristaeus. Neither of these texts survived, possibly because by 200 B.C.E. they were superseded by Apollonius's *Conics*, the definitive work on the subject. Euclid's *Surface Loci* was a two-volume work about the geometry of spheres, cones, cylinders, tori, ellipsoids and other surfaces of revolution obtained by rotating a two-dimensional figure about a line known as its axis of revolution. In this work, he discussed curves drawn on such surfaces, as well as the properties of the surfaces themselves. *Elements of Music* discussed the mathematical basis for musical theory, including Pythagoras's ratios for the notes of the musical scale. *Pseudaria* (Book of fallacies) presented a collection of incorrect proofs and common mistakes in logical reasoning from elementary geometry. *Porisms* was a three-volume work containing 38 lemmas and 171 theorems showing how to construct a point, line, or geometrical figure possessing desired properties. Examples of these types of problems included how to find the center of a circle and how to draw a circle that touched three other given circles. Historians discovered additional books on mechanics and music that may have been Euclid's work, but mathematicians who analyzed the style in which they were written believe strongly that other contemporary Greek writers created them.

Conclusion

In the eighth century, when the books written by generations of Greek mathematicians were translated into the Arabic language, Euclid's name was translated as Uclides. When historians discovered these Arabic texts, they noticed that this name was a combination of the Arabic words *ucli*, meaning "key," and *des*, meaning "measure." Some scholars wondered if it was merely a coincidence that the most influential book on geometry, the study of measurement, was written by a man whose name meant "the key to measuring" or if the works of Euclid had been created by a group of mathematicians who published their joint writings under this pen name. Although most mathematicians and historians doubt this theory of group authorship, it has occurred at other times in the history of mathematics. For 300 years after Pythagoras's death, his followers continued to give him credit for all their mathematical discoveries, and in the 20th century, a group of French mathematicians published their joint writings under the name Bourbaki.

Although this theory suggests an interesting possibility, mathematicians are almost certain that there was a real person named Euclid who wrote *Elements*, taught at the Museum of Alexandria, and ultimately died in Alexandria around 270 B.C.E. His masterpiece, *Elements*, defined the teaching of geometry for 2,000 years. Euclid's insistence that all mathematical theorems be proven logically from first principles continues to influence the way mathematicians work today.

At the end of all his proofs, Euclid would write three words meaning "that which was to be proved." In Latin, these words translate as *quod erat demonstrandum*. As a tribute to Euclid, many mathematicians today continue the tradition of ending their proofs with the abbreviation of this Latin phrase—QED.

FURTHER READING

Bulmer-Thomas, Ivor. "Euclid." In *Dictionary of Scientific Biography.* Vol. 4, edited by Charles C. Gillispie, 414–437. New York: Scribner, 1972. Encyclopedic biography.

Heath, Sir Thomas L. "Chapter 11. Euclid." In *A History of Greek Mathematics.* Vol. 1, *From Thales to Euclid*, 354–446. New York: Dover, 1981. An in-depth look at Euclid's mathematical work.

———. *The Thirteen Books of Euclid's "Elements."* 3 vols. New York: Dover, 1956. Translations with commentary of Euclid's book on algebra, number theory, and geometry.

O'Connor, J. J., and E. F. Robertson. "Euclid of Alexandria." In "MacTutor History of Mathematics Archive." University of Saint Andrews. Available online. URL: http://turnbull.mcs.st-and .ac.uk/~history/Mathematicians/Euclid.html. Accessed March

25, 2005. Online biography, from the University of Saint Andrews, Scotland.

Petechuk, David A. "Euclid of Alexandria." In *Notable Mathematicians from Ancient Times to the Present*, edited by Robin V. Young, 165–167. Detroit: Gale, 1998. Brief biography.

Reimer, Luetta, and Wilbert Reimer. "There's Only One Road: Euclid." In *Mathematicians Are People, Too: Stories from the Lives of Great Mathematicians*. Vol. 2. 1–7. Parsippany, N.J.: Seymour, 1995. Life story with historical facts and fictionalized dialogue; intended for elementary school students.

Turnbull, Herbert W. "Chapter 3. Alexandria: Euclid, Archimedes and Apollonius." In *The Great Mathematicians*, 34–47. New York: New York University Press, 1961. Contains a description of Euclid's *Elements*.

4

Archimedes of Syracuse

(ca. 287–212 B.C.E.)

Archimedes of Syracuse used the method of exhaustion to estimate perimeters, areas, and volumes of objects with curved sides. *(Library of Congress, Prints and Photographs Division)*

Innovator of Techniques in Geometry

Archimedes (pronounced ark-i-MEED-eez) of Syracuse established a reputation as an inventor of practical machines but became more famous for his discoveries in mathematics and physics. He developed the method of exhaustion to estimate perimeters, areas, and volumes. Using the Archimedean spiral, he determined tangent lines and trisected angles. Employing experimental techniques, he established theoretical principles about levers, pulleys, and centers of mass. His discovery of the principle of buoyancy established the theory of hydrostatics.

Inventor of Practical Machines

Archimedes was born ca. 287 B.C.E. in the city of Syracuse, an independent Greek city-state on the island of Sicily, off the southwestern coast of Italy. In this cultured city, Archimedes' father, Pheidias, was well known as a respected astronomer. As the son of a scientist and a member of the upper class, Archimedes received a good education. After completing his formal studies in the local schools of Syracuse, he traveled to Alexandria, the great center of learning in Egypt. There he studied under the mathematician-astronomer Canon and the mathematician Eratosthenes, who was head of the Alexandrian library. In this scholarly environment, Archimedes became interested in using mathematics to solve practical problems and in developing new mathematical ideas.

Archimedes quickly established his reputation as a creative inventor. Observing that farmers living near the Nile River did not have an efficient system for drawing water from the river, he designed a large screw enclosed in a long cylinder with a hand crank attached to one end. When the device was placed at an angle with its lower end submerged in water, the spiraling motion of the screw carried water through the device and out the upper end. Egyptian farmers used the water screw, or Archimedean screw, to draw water from the river to irrigate their crops. Various designs of this invention were used throughout the Greek world to drain water from swamps, to empty groundwater from mines, and to pump seawater from the holds of ships.

After living for a number of years in Alexandria, Archimedes returned to Syracuse, where he continued to invent machines and to study the mathematical principles that made them work. Two of the mechanical devices he studied in great detail were levers and pulleys. A lever is a long pole that rests on a pivot point. By pushing down on one end, a person would be able to lift a heavy object on the other end. A seesaw, a crowbar, and the oars of a rowboat are examples of levers. A pulley is a rope wrapped around a wheel. By pulling down on one end, a person is able to lift a heavy object tied to the other end. The rope on a flagpole, a bicycle chain, and a window washer's hoist are examples of pulleys. People had used levers and pulleys for hundreds of years before Archimedes was born, but he was the first person to fully understand the mathematical principles that made these simple machines work. He demonstrated these theories by building intricate machines using combinations of many pulleys and levers that worked in a predictable and exact manner.

Archimedes was so confident of the power of levers and pulleys that he claimed that he could move any object, no matter how heavy it was. He boasted "Give me a place to stand and I will move the earth." His friend King Hieron, the ruler of Syracuse, challenged him to launch a warship loaded with supplies and soldiers. Archimedes rigged up an intricate system of pulleys and levers and, with the slightest effort, set the huge ship into motion to the amazement of the king and the crowd of spectators who witnessed the remarkable feat.

King Hieron asked Archimedes to invent weapons that could be used to defend the walled city of Syracuse from the frequent attacks of the Roman armies. Using the principles of levers and pulleys, Archimedes invented adjustable catapults that could throw 500-pound stones over the walls of the city onto ships entering the

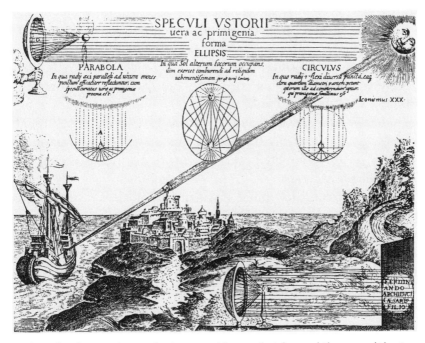

Archimedes designed curved mirrors and lenses that focused the rays of the Sun onto the sails of Roman ships, setting them on fire. *(The Granger Collection)*

harbor. He invented huge cranes that could reach over the walls, lift ships out of the water, and drop them back down to sink them. Archimedes devised machines that could shoot many arrows at once. He even invented mirrors and lenses in the shapes of paraboloids, ellipsoids, and hemispheres that could be used to focus the rays of the Sun onto the sails of ships to set them on fire. The Roman soldiers became so terrified of Archimedes' weapons that if they saw a rope hanging over the walls of the city, they would turn and retreat in fear that it might be another of his war machines.

Approximation of Pi Using Inscribed and Circumscribed Polygons

Although Archimedes became famous throughout the Roman Empire for inventing the water screw and many war machines, his mathematical discoveries were much more important. He wrote more than 20 books about his discoveries in diverse branches of mathematics and physics. His book *Measurement of the Circle* introduced new geometrical techniques for calculating distances and areas. *Sand Reckoner* presented innovative strategies to solve arithmetic problems with large numbers. *On Floating Bodies* explained his principle of buoyancy. These books and eight others have been preserved through Arabic and Latin translations. Unfortunately, at least 15 additional books that were mentioned in the writings of other mathematicians and scientists have been lost through the years. Some of his discoveries are known only because he wrote about them in letters that he sent to his friends Canon and Eratosthenes in Egypt.

One of Archimedes' finest mathematical achievements was his perfection of the method of exhaustion. Originally developed in the fifth century B.C.E. by Greek mathematicians Antiphon and Hippocrates of Chios and formalized into a rigorous technique in the fourth century B.C.E. by Eudoxus of Cnidus, this method provided a systematic procedure for estimating areas and perimeters of various shapes using a sequence of simple polygons whose areas or perimeters approximated the shape being measured. Archimedes used the method of exhaustion to estimate the value of the number π (called pi). For centuries, mathematicians had known that the distance around a circle (its circumference) divided by the distance across the circle (its diameter) was a fixed ratio. Centuries later, this number came to be represented by the Greek letter π, and the relationship was expressed by the formula $\dfrac{C}{d} = \pi$ or $C = \pi \cdot d$. If a circle's diameter was one unit long (one foot, one yard, one meter), then its circumference would be π units long. Mathematicians knew that this constant π was slightly more than three but had not devised an accurate technique for determining its exact value.

Archimedes used the method of exhaustion to develop a multi-step approach to obtain good approximations for the value of π. He started by drawing a circle of diameter one and locating six equally spaced points on the circle. He connected each point to the next by a straight line to form a six-sided figure inside the circle, called an inscribed hexagon. Since this hexagon was contained inside the circle, the distance around its outer edges (its perimeter) had to be less than the circumference of the circle. Using simple ideas from geometry, he was able to calculate the perimeter of the inscribed hexagon. He knew that this value would be close to, but less than, the value of π. He used the same six points to construct a six-sided figure that was bigger than the circle. By determining the perimeter

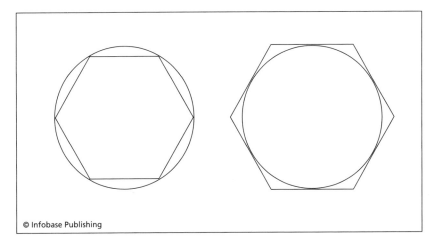

Archimedes estimated the circumference of a circle by finding the perimeters of inscribed and circumscribed polygons.

of this circumscribed hexagon, he found a number that was also close to, but greater than, the value of π. From these two hexagons, he determined that the true value of π was between 3.00 and 3.47.

He repeated this process by constructing 12-sided figures inside and outside of the circle. The perimeters of these two figures revealed that π was between 3.10 and 3.22. Repeating this process with figures having 24 sides, 48 sides, and 96 sides, he determined that π was between $3\frac{10}{71}$ and $3\frac{10}{70}$, that is between 3.1408 and 3.1429. The actual value of π cannot be expressed as a fraction, a mixed number, nor as a number with finitely many decimal places; the digits after the decimal point never end. To four decimal places, its value is 3.1416. Archimedes' approximation was much better than any other estimate known to the Greeks at the time. He published this technique and the numerical results in the book *Measurement of the Circle*. This book was widely circulated, translated into many languages, and used by students of mathematics throughout the Middle Ages. Influenced by Archimedes' writing, mathematicians in the next 18 centuries used this method of inscribed and circumscribed figures with more and more sides to determine the first 35 decimal places of this important number.

Method of Exhaustion to Estimate Areas and Volumes

The Greeks who lived at the time of Archimedes knew how to determine the exact area of any geometrical shape having straight sides, such as a hexagon or a trapezoid, by cutting it into a number of rectangles and triangles and adding up their areas. Using the method of exhaustion, they could estimate the areas of figures having curved edges by finding the areas of a sequence of simple geometrical shapes that more closely approximated the shape being measured. Archimedes explained how to use this technique to find the area inside a curve by cutting the figure into slices of equal thickness and fitting into each slice a rectangle that was as large as possible. He used the sum of the areas of these rectangles as a first estimate for the area

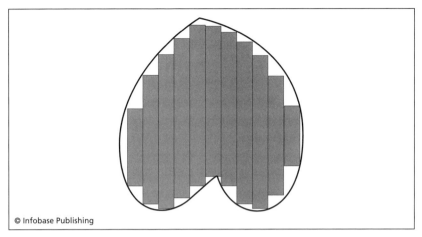

© Infobase Publishing

Archimedes used the method of exhaustion with a sequence of rectangles to estimate areas of regions with curved boundaries.

inside the curve. Repeating the cutting process with each slice only half as thick as before allowed him to create twice as many thinner rectangles whose areas generated a better estimate for the area inside the curve. By continuing this process as many times as desired, one could estimate the area inside the curve to any degree of accuracy.

In his mathematical writings, Archimedes described three variations of the method of exhaustion using differences, ratios, and approximations of areas and used them to prove a large number of theorems. In his book *On the Quadrature of the Parabola*, he used the method of exhaustion with triangular approximations to determine the area of a segment of a parabola. In another book, *On Conoids and Spheroids*, he showed how to use the method of exhaustion to determine the area inside an ellipse. In the previously mentioned book *Measurement of the Circle*, he used the differences between the areas of inscribed and circumscribed polygons to show that the area of a circle was equal to the area of a triangle whose height was the same as the radius of the circle and whose base was equal to the circumference of the circle. Since the area of a triangle is $\frac{1}{2}$(base)(height), he showed that the area of the circle was $\frac{1}{2}(r)(2\pi r)$, which is the familiar formula $A = \pi r^2$.

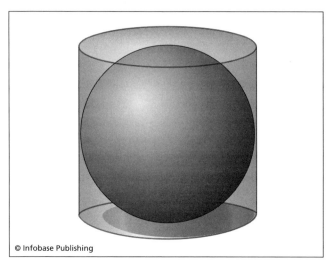

Archimedes was most proud of his proof that the volume of a sphere is two-thirds of the volume of the cylinder that contains it.

Archimedes used a modified version of the method of exhaustion to find the surface areas and volumes of three-dimensional objects that had curved surfaces, such as spheres, cones, and cylinders. He presented these results in his book *On the Sphere and the Cylinder*, which he regarded as his favorite among all of his books. He used the method of exhaustion with ratios of triangular areas to find the surface area of a cone. To find the volume of a sphere, he cut the sphere into slices that were the same thickness and fit into each slice the largest possible disk. Since the volume of a disk was easy to calculate, he was able to estimate the volume of the sphere by adding up the volumes of the disks. With thinner and thinner slices, the disks gave better and better estimates, and he eventually determined that a sphere with radius r had a volume of $V = \frac{4}{3}\pi r^3$.

When he discovered this volume formula, Archimedes realized that if the sphere was enclosed in the smallest possible cylinder, like a ball fitting snuggly into a can, the volume of the sphere was two-thirds of the volume of the cylinder. With additional calculations, he discovered that the surface area of the sphere was also two-thirds of the surface area of the cylinder; that is, $A = 4\pi r^2$. Archimedes considered this pair of discoveries to be the greatest achievement of his life. He was so fascinated by these results that he requested that a picture of a sphere inside a cylinder be engraved on his tombstone along with the fraction $\frac{2}{3}$. Although the location of his grave is no longer known, the Roman historian Cicero wrote that in 75 B.C.E. he had found the location and seen the legendary engraving on the tombstone.

Archimedes was intrigued by the mathematical properties of everyday objects. He studied the surface areas of the curved knives called *arbelos* used by shoemakers and the traditionally shaped bowls called *salinon* that Greeks used to hold table salt. While investigating volumes, he noticed that if a sphere, such as an orange, was cut into slices that had the same thickness, then each slice would have the same amount of orange peel as well. It did not matter if it was cut from the end of the orange or the middle of the orange. If there were 10 slices all having the same thickness, then each piece would have $\frac{1}{10}$th of the orange peel. He presented his analysis of these interesting shapes in his *Book of Lemmas*. In his extensive use of the method of exhaustion to find perimeters, areas, and volumes of curved objects, he developed most of the fundamental concepts of integration, one of the two major ideas in calculus.

Creative Problem-Solver

As a practical scientist, Archimedes found the inspiration for many of his ideas by experimenting with physical models of the objects that he was studying. He would cut out a piece of metal in a particular shape and try to balance it on a stick to find its central axis, spin it on his fingertip to find its center of mass, and weigh it to find its area. With the observations that he made from these informal experiments, he was able to get an idea of what the mathematical solution might be. This experimental approach was radically different from the way that other mathematicians of his time worked. Following the teachings of the great philosopher Plato, they regarded abstract mathematics as the only real path to knowledge. They believed that the physical world and practical experiments would not lead to wisdom and truth. Archimedes was much freer with his thinking and was open to learning how things worked by observing the world around him. In one of his first books, the two-volume work *On the Equilibrium of Planes*, Archimedes presented his discoveries about the laws of levers and the centers of mass of various polygons. As he did in most of his books, he presented only the elegant proofs of his theories without explaining how he had discovered these principles. In the later book *On the Method of Mechanical Theorems*, usually called *The Method*, he described the experimental processes through which he got many of his ideas that he then developed into mathematical theories. This book allowed readers to understand the workings of his brilliant and creative mind.

One of Archimedes' most difficult and important books was *On Spirals*. In this book, he investigated a curve that has come to be known as the Archimedean spiral. This curve starts at a point (called its origin) and expands at a steady rate as it spins around. The formula describing such a curve is $r = a\theta$. Since a spiral could not be created using only a ruler and a compass, the mathematicians who followed Plato's teachings refused to use it to solve problems. Archimedes discovered how to use this spiral to cut any angle into three equal angles—a famous problem called trisecting an angle that mathematicians had been trying to solve for hundreds of years. He was also able to find the equation of the line that was tangent at any point on a spiral curve. A tangent line touches the curve at a specified place and points in the same direction that the curve is headed. Tangent lines incorporate the fundamental concept of the derivative—the second of the two major ideas of modern calculus. With tangent lines and the method of exhaustion, Archimedes almost invented this important area of mathematics 18 centuries before it was eventually discovered by Sir Isaac Newton and Gottfried Leibniz.

Many times during his life, Archimedes demonstrated that he had an incredible ability to see things in a way that no one else did. Part of this ability came from his intense powers of concentration. He was able to block out all distractions and think deeply about a problem for long periods of time. While sitting by the fire on a cold evening, he would often rake some ashes from the fire, spread them on the floor and start drawing diagrams in them to solve a problem that he had been thinking about for days. After taking a bath, Greeks usually rubbed oil all over their bodies. While rubbing in the oil, Archimedes would frequently draw mathematical shapes on his skin with his fingernails as he continued thinking about an idea that had interested him.

King Hieron asked Archimedes to determine whether his new crown was made from pure gold or if the craftsman had cheated him by substituting some less valuable metal for a portion of the gold. The crown weighed as much as the amount of gold that the craftsman had been given, but no one could think of a way to determine if the crown was pure gold without destroying it. While getting into the tub for his bath, Archimedes noticed that the level of the water rose as he sat down into it, and as more of his body went into the water, the water rose higher and higher. He realized that like any object, his body was replacing an amount of water that was equal to the space it took up (its volume). Archimedes knew he could use this idea to solve the problem about the king's crown. In his excitement over this sudden realization, he jumped from the tub and, without grabbing his towel or putting on his clothes, he ran through the streets shouting "Eureka!" meaning "I have found it!"

When Archimedes arrived at the king's palace, he put the king's crown into a bowl of water and measured how much the water rose. Then he submerged an amount of gold that weighed the same as the crown. When the water did not rise as high as it had with the crown, he was able to determine that the crown was not made of pure gold. One reason that Archimedes was able to make so many discoveries was that his mind was always alert for little hints that gave him the insight to solve big problems.

What Archimedes discovered in the tub was that, when an object is placed into a liquid, the weight of the object will be reduced by the weight of the liquid that it replaces. This principle is now known as the Archimedean Principle of Buoyancy and is a basic law in the science of hydrostatics, the area of physics that deals with properties of liquids. In his book *On Floating Bodies*, he explained the principles of buoyancy and specific gravity and gave a mathematical development of the theory of hydrostatics.

Investigations of Large Numbers

Like his father before him, Archimedes was also interested in astronomy. He constructed a model of the universe with moving parts that showed how the Sun, the Moon, the planets, and the stars moved around the Earth. This planetsphere, which was powered by flowing water, even showed eclipses of the Sun and the Moon. He calculated the distance from the Earth to each of the planets and to the Sun, as well as the size of each heavenly body. He used these measurements to prove a point to other mathematicians who insisted that there was no number large enough to count all the grains of sand on the beach. Archimedes proved them wrong by finding a number that was larger than the number of grains of sand that it would take to fill the entire universe from the Earth to the farthest stars.

In his book *Sand Reckoner*, he explained the process by which he made this huge calculation. He first determined how many grains of sand would equal the size of a poppy seed. Then he estimated how many poppy seeds would equal the size of a finger. Continuing this process, he estimated how many fingers would fill a stadium, how many stadiums would fill a larger space, and so on. Archimedes invented names and notations for these large numbers. By multiplying all these numbers together, he obtained a result that was in the "seventh power of a myriad-myriads." The technique he used to write down such a large number provided the basic idea that other mathematicians used many years later to invent our current exponential and scientific notations. Today we would recognize this huge number as 10^{63}, a one followed by 63 zeros.

Archimedes became famous for his ability to solve complicated problems. His reputation was so widespread that whenever someone had a difficult problem to solve, especially one that involved large numbers, they would call it an Archimedean problem. The name implied that the problem was so hard that it would take someone as brilliant as Archimedes to solve it. One such problem was the Cattle Problem, which involved eight variables representing the number of cows and bulls of four different colors that satisfied eight equations. The solution involves eight numbers that are so large that it would take 600 pages to write them down. Archimedes included the statement of this problem, without its solution, and other similar "recreational" problems in his *Book of Lemmas*.

Less than half of the books Archimedes wrote have survived through the years. He wrote books on various topics in geometry— *On Touching Circles, On Parallel Lines, On Triangles, On the Properties of the Right Triangle, On the Division of the Circle into Seven Equal Parts,* and *On Polyhedra*—that are known only because they are mentioned in the writings of other mathematicians. Several of his scientific books—*Elements of Mechanics, On Balances, On Uprights, On Blocks and Cylinders,* and *Catoptrics*—were cited by other scholars but have been lost. A number of works on other topics—*On Data, The Naming of Numbers,* and *On Water Clocks*—are also missing.

In 1906, while examining a 12th-century prayer book, a researcher discovered some faint writing in the background that had been partially erased from the parchment. He determined that the underlying text was a 10th-century copy of several of Archimedes' works, including portions of *The Method.* This 174-page book known as Archimedes' Palimpsest is the oldest-existing copy of his written works. In 1998, an anonymous billionaire bought the rare book at an auction for $2 million and loaned it to the Walters Art Museum in Baltimore, Maryland, where researchers continue to clean, preserve, and translate it.

In 212 b.c.e., when Archimedes was 75 years old, the Roman army finally conquered Syracuse. On the day of the Roman invasion, Archimedes was one of the only residents not celebrating at a festival. He was drawing a diagram in the sand to solve a math problem when a soldier ordered him to get up and come with him. Archimedes told the soldier to move out of his light and wait until he finished solving the problem. The impatient and angry soldier killed Archimedes with his spear.

Conclusion

During his career, Archimedes solved almost all of the major problems in mathematics that had been unanswered at the time. With his perfection of the method of exhaustion to estimate areas and his use of the spiral to determine tangent lines, he came very close to inventing calculus 18 centuries before it was ultimately discovered. The experimental approach he used to attack geometry problems challenged the accepted wisdom of his day. His work with curved areas and surfaces advanced tremendously the state of geometry. The calculations he performed with very small and very large numbers introduced new techniques in arithmetic. Because his many original and significant discoveries demonstrated such powerful insight, mathematicians rank Archimedes with Sir Isaac Newton and Carl Friedrich Gauss as one of the three greatest mathematicians of all time.

FURTHER READING

Clagett, Marshall. "Archimedes." In *Dictionary of Scientific Biography.* Vol. 1, edited by Charles C. Gillispie, 213–231. New York: Scribner, 1972. Detailed encyclopedic biography.

Heath, Sir Thomas L. "Chapter 13. Archimedes." In *A History of Greek Mathematics.* Vol. 2, *From Aristarchus to Diophantus,* 16–109. New York: Dover, 1981. An in-depth look at Archimedes' mathematical work.

Heath, Sir Thomas L., ed. *The Works of Archimedes.* New York: Dover, 1953. Translations with commentary of the extant works of Archimedes, including the Palimpsest.

O'Connor, J. J., and E. F. Robertson. "Archimedes of Syracuse." In "MacTutor History of Mathematics Archive." University of Saint Andrews. Available online. URL: http://turnbull.mcs.st-and.ac.uk/~history/Mathematicians/Archimedes.html. Accessed March 25, 2005. Online biography, from the University of Saint Andrews, Scotland.

Reimer, Luetta, and Wilbert Reimer. "The Man Who Concentrated Too Hard: Archimedes." In *Mathematicians Are People, Too: Stories from the Lives of Great Mathematicians,* 18–28. Parsippany, N.J.: Seymour, 1990. Life story with historical facts and fictionalized dialogue; intended for elementary school students.

Reinherz, Leslie. "Archimedes of Syracuse." In *Notable Mathematicians from Ancient Times to the Present,* edited by Robin V. Young, 15–17. Detroit: Gale, 1998. Brief biography.

"The Archimedes Palimpsest." NOVA Infinite Secrets. Available online. URL: http://www.pbs.org/wgbh/nova/archimedes/palimpsest.html. Accessed March 28, 2005. Online notes and photos of the palimpsest manuscript, with links to the related episode of the NOVA television show, from the Public Broadcasting System.

Turnbull, Herbert W. "Chapter 3. Alexandria: Euclid, Archimedes and Apollonius." In *The Great Mathematicians,* 34–47. New York: New York University Press, 1961. An overview of Archimedes' mathematical works.

Hypatia of Alexandria

5

(ca. 370–415 C.E.)

Hypatia of Alexandria wrote commentaries on classic mathematical works. *(Library of Congress, Prints and Photographs Division)*

First Woman of Mathematics

The Greek mathematician and philosopher Hypatia (pronounced hi-PAY-shuh) of Alexandria is the first woman known to have taught and written about mathematics. Her commentaries enhanced and preserved classic works of ancient mathematicians. She was a Neo-Platonist philosopher, a teacher of mathematics, and a respected scientist. Her brutal murder by an angry mob marked the end of seven centuries of intellectual culture in Alexandria, Egypt.

The "Perfect" Human Being

Hypatia was born in the city of Alexandria, Egypt, during the last half of the fourth century. The details of her life are known primarily from four sources: *The Letters of Synesius of Cyrene*, which includes several pieces of correspondence from her student Synesius; an excerpt from the historian Socrates Scholasticus' fifth-century work *Ecclesiastical History*; an entry in *The Chronicle of John, Coptic Bishop of Nikiu*, written in the seventh century; and a passage from the 10th-century encyclopedia *Suda Lexicon*. The conflicting information from these historical records places her date of birth between 350 and 370 c.e.

Seven centuries earlier, when the warrior-king Alexander the Great conquered the kingdom of Egypt, he decided to build a great city at the mouth of the Nile River. He designed the city to be a military stronghold, a hub of international commerce, and the world's greatest center of knowledge and learning. He and his successor, Ptolemy I, built a large library with the goal of collecting every book that had ever been written. They established a policy that whenever learned people came to Alexandria, their books would be brought to the library, where scribes would make handwritten copies of them. The copies were then placed in the library, where they were made available to the public. Ptolemy also established the Museum of Alexandria as a university where scholars from every country could gather to discuss, learn, teach, and discover new ideas. Many important discoveries were made by Greek mathematicians living and working in Alexandria.

Hypatia's parents were among the well-educated citizens of Greece who were attracted to this beautiful city at the center of the civilized world. Her father, Theon, was a professor of mathematics and astronomy at the museum. In addition to teaching, he wrote about eclipses of the Sun and the Moon and edited existing mathematics and astronomy textbooks to make the material more accessible to his students. He was eventually appointed to the position of director of the museum. Hypatia was an only child; her mother died when she was very young.

Theon devoted himself to the idealistic goal of raising his daughter to become the "perfect" human being, enabling her to reach the full potential of her physical, mental, and spiritual abilities. Following a fitness routine that her father had devised for her, Hypatia spent many hours each day running, hiking, horseback riding, rowing, and swimming. Theon often accompanied her in these physical activities. Her father also designed a challenging educational program to develop her mental abilities. Under his instruction, Hypatia learned to read and write, do math and science, debate, and speak in front of an audience. Accompanying her father to the museum each day, she read the classic works of Greek literature and was exposed to the ideas of the ancient philosophers and scholars.

In the environment that the museum, library, and city provided to her, Hypatia became an excellent public speaker and excelled in mathematics and philosophy—the study of the meaning of life. To complement her academic education, she traveled to Greece and to other countries around the Mediterranean Sea. As she visited these countries and met many new people, she developed an understanding of various cultures and a respect for different traditions and points of view.

Commentaries on Classical Mathematics Books

When she returned to Alexandria, Hypatia joined her father at the museum, where she taught courses in mathematics and philosophy. Although she rapidly established her reputation as an excellent teacher and attracted a loyal following of students, her mathematical writings had a greater impact on future generations of students. Hypatia worked with her father to revise and update classic mathematics texts. In her time, these were called "commentaries"; today such works would be called "edited versions." Writers of commentaries made corrections, revised some explanations, and added material that had originally been presented in other books that were no longer available. They updated the books by including new discoveries that had been made since the time that the books had first been written. Hypatia, Theon, and other professors used these new books to teach their students at the museum. Traveling scholars brought copies of the commentaries to universities in other countries, where they were translated into Latin, Arabic, and other languages.

Hypatia and Theon worked together to produce a commentary on Euclid's *Elements*. This book, considered by academic scholars to be the most influential textbook ever written, had been created 700 years earlier by the museum's first mathematics professor, the Greek scholar Euclid. In 13 chapters that Euclid called "books," he had logically and systematically presented all the elementary mathematics that was known at the time so university students could study from a single textbook. Theon and Hypatia corrected mistakes that had been made in earlier copies of the book and expanded some explanations to make the material easier to understand. They also hoped to preserve this mathematical knowledge for future generations. The edition of *Elements* that they prepared was so highly regarded that it became the standard edition of the text for the next thousand years. Although hundreds of versions of Euclid's *Elements* were prepared by other mathematicians throughout the centuries, Theon and Hypatia's edition remained the one most frequently used and was considered to be the most faithful to the original manuscript.

Independent of her father, Hypatia wrote commentaries on three other mathematics books—Diophantus's *Arithmetic*, Ptolemy's *Handy Tables*, and Apollonius's *Conics*. In these important mathematical works from three different centuries, each author had presented the most advanced knowledge in a particular branch of mathematics. Hypatia's broad understanding of mathematics and its applications, as well as her experience as a teacher, enabled her to improve upon the versions of these works that existed in her day.

Hypatia's first commentary was on the book *Arithmetic*. Written by the Greek mathematician Diophantus around the year 250, this book presented a collection of 150 word problems drawn from all areas of mathematics. After stating each problem, the author presented one or more mathematical equations that represented the relationships between the unknown quantities and gave a method of solution using techniques from algebra. In this book, Diophantus introduced a systematic notation for representing exponents beyond the square and cube as well as a method for dealing with coefficients. Hypatia added two types of material to Diophantus's work. She included a technique for solving a pair of simultaneous equations—two equations relating the same variables that needed to be solved at the same time. In modern algebraic notation, the system of equations is represented as $x - y = a$ and $x^2 - y^2 = m(x - y) + b$ for specified values of the constants a, b, and m. Historians do not know whether she invented this method or whether it was discovered by other mathematicians after *Arithmetic* was first written. She also added steps at the end of many problems showing readers how to verify that their solutions were correct.

Hypatia wrote another commentary on the book *The Astronomical Canon* that had been written by the astronomer Ptolemy around the year 150. This book, also published under the title *Handy Tables*, contained lists that gave the lengths of the arcs of a circle that were cut out by angles as small as $\dfrac{1}{3600}$ of a degree. These calculations were used by astronomers, sailors, land surveyors, and others whose work involved geometry. Theon, who had published an earlier commentary on these tables, stated that the quality of his daughter's work surpassed his own. Historians disagree about whether Theon's praise for Hypatia's work was sincere or whether he was attempting to enhance her reputation as a scholar.

The third commentary written by Hypatia was on the book *Conics* that had been written by the Greek mathematician Apollonius around 200 B.C.E. This book described how the three important curved shapes—the ellipse, the parabola, and the hyperbola—could be obtained by slicing a double cone with a flat plane. An ellipse describes the orbit of a planet around the Sun as well as the path traveled by an electron in an atom. A parabola is the shape used to design reflectors for flashlights and cables for suspension bridges. Hyperbolas

Apollonius's *Conics* was one of three classic works for which Hypatia produced a valuable commentary. *(Library of Congress, Prints and Photographs Division)*

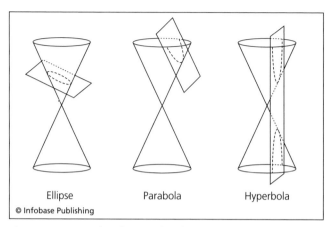

Ellipse   Parabola   Hyperbola

© Infobase Publishing

The intersection of a plane and a double cone will produce one of three conic sections—ellipse, parabola, or hyperbola.

are used in the design of cooling towers at power plants; they also describe the paths of some comets. All three curves are used in the design of antennae, telescope lenses, and television satellite dishes. This book remained the most advanced work on these important curves for another 1,300 years.

Famous Teacher, Philosopher, and Scientist

In addition to becoming well respected for her mathematical writings, Hypatia developed a reputation as an excellent speaker and teacher. She gave public lectures and private lessons on mathematics and philosophy. When she taught or spoke, Hypatia would dress in the long, flowing robes traditionally worn by philosophers of her time. She taught her students to have respect for different perspectives and competing points of view on controversial issues. Her teachings on philosophy incorporated the ideas of Plato, who encouraged people to seek knowledge and to develop their spiritual side, as well as the ideas of Aristotle, who emphasized logic and the analysis of the physical world.

After earning a strong reputation as a teacher at the museum, Hypatia became the head of another school in Alexandria—the

Neo-Platonic School of Philosophy. Neo-Platonists believed that the goal of life was to focus less on the physical world of the body and more on the higher spiritual world of the mind and the soul. People traveled to Alexandria from many different countries to hear Hypatia speak and to learn from her. Her home and her school became gathering places where educated people discussed and learned mathematics and philosophy.

In Alexandria at the time of Hypatia, many women were well educated, but few women taught at universities, and it was very rare for a woman to be a leader in her field. Hypatia's accomplishments as a respected leader in two fields—mathematics and philosophy— indicated her stature as a leading intellectual of her era.

Hypatia was also a respected member of her community. She was asked by friends to speak to government officials on behalf of needy people. The citizens of Alexandria knew her to be a generous, kind, and caring individual. She never married, freeing her to devote her life to writing, teaching, and works of charity.

Hypatia was also a capable scientist who possessed practical skills. She designed two scientific instruments for her friend and former student Synesius, who eventually became the Christian bishop of the city of Ptolemais. A collection of the letters that he wrote to friends and colleagues was published as *The Letters of Synesius of Cyrene*. In his letters to Hypatia, Synesius thanked her for designing an astrolabe and a hydrometer for him. An astrolabe was an instrument used by sailors to determine a ship's location by measuring the positions of the stars. Hypatia did not invent the first astrolabe; it had already been in use for a hundred years. As a scientist and teacher, Hypatia was able to clearly explain to her friend the instructions for making and using an astrolabe. A hydrometer was an instrument that measured how heavy a liquid was compared to an equal volume of water. Historians believe that Synesius probably used the hydrometer that Hypatia designed for him to mix his own medicines or to diagnose his health problems.

Brutally Murdered

By the early fifth century, the city of Alexandria became involved in rapid social changes. The Museum of Alexandria, its valuable collection of books, and the intellectual culture that surrounded it were no longer priorities for the Romans who ruled Egypt nor for the residents of Alexandria. Political leaders struggling to maintain their authority felt threatened by the large groups of enthusiastic followers who attended private meetings at Hypatia's home, lectures at her school, and speeches that she gave in public gatherings throughout the city. Local leaders of the Christian and Jewish churches thought that her mathematical and scientific ideas contradicted the teachings of their religions and that her philosophical ideas were attracting the followers of their religions.

In 415, Hypatia became entangled in a dispute between a group of Christians led by Cyril, the archbishop of Alexandria, and the supporters of Orestes, the government prefect of Alexandria. After many members of both groups suffered violent deaths, the feud reached its peak. As Hypatia was riding through the streets of Alexandria in her chariot on her way to giving a speech, an angry mob surrounded her. They dragged her from her chariot, beat her, and threw her to the ground. They tore off her clothes, cut her body into pieces, and burned them. The dispute was

An angry mob dragged Hypatia from her chariot and murdered her. *(ARPL/ Topham/The Image Works)*

promptly settled, but no one was ever arrested nor punished for this violent incident.

Conclusion

Hypatia's death marked the end of the era of intellectual enlightenment and the advancement of knowledge that had thrived in Alexandria for 750 years. After she was murdered, many scholars left the city and moved to Athens or to other centers of learning. In the next decades, foreign invaders and rebellious citizens attacked the buildings of the great university and vandalized the library, burning many books to heat the water at the public baths. Theon and Hypatia's version of Euclid's *Elements* and Hypatia's commentaries on Diophantus's *Arithmetic*, Ptolemy's *Handy Tables*, and Apollonius's *Conics* were preserved only through the copies that had been brought by scholars to cities in the Near East, where they were translated into Arabic. Any philosophical writings that she may have created were permanently lost.

Hypatia's uniqueness as an intellectual woman in a male-dominated culture and the violent manner of her death have caused her story to be retold by historians and writers through the centuries. Historical texts from the fifth, seventh, and 10th centuries tell the story of her life and death and of her contributions to mathematics and philosophy. In 1851, English novelist C. Kingsley dramatized the story of Hypatia's life and of her murder in his book *Hypatia*. Brief biographical portraits were included in popular collections of short stories such as E. Hubbard's 1908 book *Little Journeys to the Homes of Great Teachers*. In the 1980s, modern-day scholars established the journal *Hypatia*, in which they publish scholarly papers written by women about issues in philosophy and women's studies.

FURTHER READING

Carpenter, Jill. "Hypatia of Alexandria." In *Notable Mathematicians from Ancient Times to the Present*, edited by Robin V. Young, 257–259. Detroit: Gale, 1998. Brief biography.

Dzielska, Maria. *Hypatia of Alexandria*. Cambridge, Mass.: Harvard University Press, 1995. Book-length biography of the philosopher-mathematician.

Koch, Laura Coffin. "Hypatia." In *Notable Women in Mathematics: A Biographical Dictionary,* edited by Charlene Morrow and Teri Perl, 94–97. Westport, Conn.: Greenwood Press, 1998. Short biography.

Kramer, Edna E. "Hypatia." In *Dictionary of Scientific Biography.* Vol. 6, edited by Charles C. Gillispie, 615–616. New York: Scribner, 1972. Brief encyclopedic biography.

Mueller, Ian. "Hypatia." In *Women of Mathematics: A Biobibliographic Sourcebook,* edited by Louise S. Grinstein and Paul J. Campbell, 74–79. New York: Greenwood Press, 1987. Addresses her life and work with an extensive list of references.

O'Connor, J. J., and E. F. Robertson. "Hypatia of Alexandria." In "MacTutor History of Mathematics Archive." University of Saint Andrews. Available online. URL: http://turnbull.mcs.st-and .ac.uk/~history/Mathematicians/Hypatia.html. Accessed March 25, 2005. Online biography, from the University of Saint Andrews, Scotland.

Osen, Lynn M. "Hypatia." In *Women in Mathematics,* 21–32. Cambridge, Mass.: MIT Press, 1974. Detailed biography.

Perl, Teri. "Hypatia." In *Math Equals: Biographies of Women Mathematicians + Related Activities,* 8–27. Menlo Park, Calif.: Addison-Wesley, 1978. Detailed biography accompanied by exercises related to her mathematical work.

Reimer, Luetta, and Wilbert Reimer. "A Woman of Courage: Hypatia." In *Mathematicians Are People, Too: Stories from the Lives of Great Mathematicians,* 28–35. Parsippany, N.J.: Seymour, 1990. Life story with historical facts and fictionalized dialogue, intended for elementary school students.

6

Āryabhata I

(476–550 c.e.)

Āryabhata wrote an influential treatise on mathematics and astronomy. *(Dinodia/The Image Works)*

From Alphabetical Numbers to the Rotation of the Earth

Āryabhata I (pronounced AR-yah-BAH-tah) wrote one of India's most enduring treatises on mathematics and astronomy. The alphabetical system of notation he developed used combinations of consonants and vowels to represent large numbers. He presented efficient methods for calculating cube roots, formulas for summing series of numbers, and algebraic methods for solving indeterminate linear equations. The table of sines and the estimate for π that he promoted remained in use for centuries. In astronomy, he proposed the controversial theory that the Earth rotated on its axis, gave accurate estimates for the length of a year, and presented formulas to calculate the orbits of the planets. India paid tribute to his achievements by naming their first satellite in his honor.

According to an autobiographical notation in one of his books, Āryabhata was born in 476 C.E. in India. Conflicting historical sources and traditions disagree about the place of his birth, suggesting several locations, including Kerala, Ashmaka, Tamil Nadu, Andhra Pradesh, Kusumapura, and Pātaliputra. During most of his professional life, he lived in Kusumapura, the mathematical center of northern India. The ruler of the Gupta dynasty appointed him director of Nalanda University, where he had studied as a young man. His titles Āryabhata I or Āryabhata the Elder distinguish him from the mathematician of the same name who lived four centuries later.

Āryabhatīya (Āryabhata's Treatise)

At the age of 23, Āryabhata wrote the first of his two works on mathematics and astronomy titled *Āryabhatīya* (Āryabhata's treatise). This brief work combined his original theories and discoveries with a summary of current knowledge in the two related disciplines. He composed the work as 118 stanzas of poetry, a common style that enabled generations of mathematicians and astronomers to preserve the text accurately for centuries through oral tradition. The first of its four sections, the 10-verse *Dasagītikā* (Introduction), gave an enumeration of astronomical constants, explained an alphabetical system for representing numbers, and presented a list of sine differences. In the 33-verse *Ganitapāda* (Mathematics), he presented 66 rules to solve a variety of problems in arithmetic, geometry, algebra, and trigonometry, including summing arithmetic progressions, determining areas and volumes, solving linear equations, and using sine differences to determine the sines of angles. The 25-verse section titled *Kālakriyāpāda* (On the reckoning of time) discussed Hindu divisions of time and presented rules for computing the locations of planets. In the final section, the 50-verse *Golapāda* (On the sphere), he presented his theories about the spherical universe and the trigonometric rules needed to calculate planetary orbits and eclipses.

The *Āryabhatīya* stands out among the many Indian works on mathematics and astronomy as the oldest complete work by an identifiable author. In the 13 centuries prior to its creation, scholars had written many *sulbasutras*, in which they presented rules of arithmetic and geometry used for measuring with lengths of rope called *sulbas*, as well as numerous astronomical treatises called *siddhāntas*, in which they explained techniques for determining planetary orbits and predicting celestial events. Āryabhata assembled a concise summary of the most important and useful material from this rich tradition and incorporated his original methods and theories in mathematics and astronomy.

In addition to preserving an accurate record of the advanced state of Hindu mathematics and astronomy in the late fifth century, the *Āryabhatīya* exerted an enduring influence on the continued development of these disciplines in both India and the Arabic empire. From the sixth century through the 16th century, Hindu scholars wrote numerous commentaries elaborating on Āryabhata's work and created derivative works based on his treatise. With a few corrected geometrical formulas and some revised astronomical theories, teachers and scholars continued to use the work for a thousand years. In the eighth century, Muslim scholars who referred to Āryabhata as Arjabhar translated his treatise into Arabic under the title *Zīj al-Arjabhar* (Astronomical tables of Arjabhar). Mathematicians and astronomers at Baghdad's House of Wisdom drew extensively from this translation and from other works that were influenced by it as they developed their own treatises.

Arithmetical Methods

One of the innovations Āryabhata introduced in his book was an alphabetical system for representing numbers, including large powers of 10. He used the 33 consonants of the Indian alphabet to stand for the integers from 1 to 25 and the multiples of 10 from 30 to 100. A consonant followed by a vowel indicated a power of 10, enabling this system of numeration to represent numbers as large as 10^{18}. He identified these values using the traditional names, such as *sahasra*

(1,000), *ayuta* (10,000), and *niyuta* (100,000), that had appeared in older works. The ancient Vedic text *Atharveda* (Knowledge of the wise and the old) from 1000 B.C.E. had given names for each power of 10 up to 10^{12}, and the *Lalitavistara* (Voice of the Buddha) from the first century B.C.E. had given names for powers of 10 up to 10^{53}. Although the Hindus were familiar with the concept of large powers of 10, Āryabhata's alphabetical notational system provided the oldest-known method for symbolically representing such quantities.

Throughout the remainder of the book, Āryabhata carried out his computations using the base-10 place-value system of notation that had symbols for the digits from one through nine plus zero. His methods for determining square roots and cube roots of large integers were designed to work efficiently with this numbering system. In his technique for finding the cube root of a number, he explained how to organize the number's digits into groups of three and gave names to each digit within a group. He then described a repetitive process in which one subtracted the last three terms of an appropriate binomial expansion of the form $(a + b)^3 = a^3 + 3a^2b + 3ab^2 + b^3$. Although he did not mention this algebraic formula explicitly, it clearly formed the basis of his algorithm.

In another group of verses, he explained how to work with arithmetic progressions—sums of terms of the form $a + (a + d) + (a + 2d) + \ldots + (a + (n-1) \cdot d)$. He gave a formula for determining the middle term of such a series and explained how to use this result to calculate the sum of the series. As an alternative method, he offered that the

$$M = \left(\frac{n-1}{2}\right) \times d + a$$

$$S = M \times \frac{n}{2} = [(a) + (a+(n-1)d)] \times \frac{n}{2}$$

© Infobase Publishing

Āryabhata gave formulas for finding the middle term and the sum of an arithmetic series.

sum could be obtained by adding the first and last terms, then multiplying this result by half the number of terms. He also provided a more complicated formula for determining how many terms were in the series if the sum, the first term, and the common difference were known. The procedure he described indicated that he knew how to use the quadratic formula to solve second-degree equations, although the formula did not appear anywhere in the text.

After working with arithmetic series, he gave formulas for the sum of other types of series. He used calculations with compound interest to illustrate the formulas for determining sums of geometric series. After giving the formula for the sum of the first n positive integers

$1 + 2 + 3 \ldots + n = \dfrac{n(n + 1)}{2}$, he also showed how to determine the sum

of their squares $1^2 + 2^2 + 3^2 + \ldots + n^2 = \dfrac{n(n + 1)(2n + 1)}{6}$ and the sum

of their cubes $1^3 + 2^3 + 3^3 + \ldots + n^3 = \left(\dfrac{n(n + 1)}{2}\right)^2$.

Throughout his book, he concisely presented these and other formulas and examples without any proofs or rationales to justify the techniques involved.

Geometric Techniques

Āryabhata provided a collection of formulas for determining the areas and volumes of geometrical objects. He presented the well-known formula for the area of a triangle as half the product of the

base and the height, $A_{triangle} = \dfrac{1}{2}bh$. He gave the area of a circle as

the product of half the circumference and half the diameter,

$A_{circle} = \left(\dfrac{C}{2}\right)\left(\dfrac{d}{2}\right) = (\pi r)(r) = \pi r^2$, a formula mentioned in earlier

Babylonian and Chinese texts. For the area of a trapezoid, he used another familiar formula: half the sum of the two parallel sides times the length of the perpendicular between them,

$A_{trapezoid} = \dfrac{1}{2}(b_1 + b_2)h$. In contrast to these formulas for areas, his formulas for calculating the volumes of three-dimensional objects were not accurate. He specified the volume of a sphere as the area of a great circle times the square root of this area, $V_{sphere} = \pi r^2 \cdot \sqrt{\pi r^2} \approx 1.77\ \pi r^3$, a significant deviation from the correct result of $V_{sphere} = \frac{4}{3} \pi r^3 \approx 1.33\ \pi r^3$. The formula he presented for the volume of a pyramid was half the product of the base and the altitude, $V_{pyramid} = \frac{1}{2} Bh$, when the correct formula should have been a third of the product, $V_{pyramid} = \frac{1}{3} Bh$. The inexplicable mixture of correct and incorrect formulas led later critics to describe the work as a collection of common pebbles and expensive jewels.

In different parts of the book, Āryabhata gave three conflicting estimates for the value of π, the ratio of the circumference of a circle to its diameter. He stated that a circle with diameter 20,000 would have a circumference of approximately 62,832. This ratio produced the estimate $\pi = \frac{C}{d} \approx \frac{62,832}{20,000} = 3.1416$ that was accurate to four decimal places. The equivalent value $3\frac{177}{1250}$ had appeared a century earlier in the *Paulisha Siddhānta* (Astronomical treatise of Paul) that was based on the work of the astronomer Paul of Alexandria. This value represented an improvement over the estimate of $3\frac{17}{120} = 3.1416\bar{6}$ given by Ptolemy of Alexandria in the second century. Some mathematicians have interpreted Āryabhata's statement that the fraction $\frac{62,832}{20,000}$ approximated the value of π to mean that he understood that π was an irrational number whose exact value could not be expressed as a fraction of two integers. Other mathematicians are reluctant to attribute such a momentous discovery to him solely on the basis of this brief passage. Later in the text, he made extensive trigonometric computations using a circle of radius 3,438 and circumference 21,600 that implied a value of $\pi = \dfrac{C}{d} = \dfrac{12,600}{2 \cdot 3438}$.

In other calculations, he used the traditional "Indian value" of $\pi = \sqrt{10} \approx 3.1623$ that had appeared in earlier texts. After providing an excellent fractional estimate for π, his use of two less accurate approximations demonstrated a measure of inconsistency within his treatise.

The *Āryabhatīya* also included explanations of geometrical methods for determining distances using similar triangles formed by lines of sight and vertical poles called gnomons. In one example, he described the situation of two gnomons of the same known height set on level ground a fixed distance apart. These were aligned with a taller third pole topped with a light causing each gnomon to cast a shadow. Given the lengths of the shadows and the distance between the two gnomons, he explained how to find the height of the pole and its distance to the first gnomon. Writers of mathematical treatises typically included problems similar to this because the techniques used to solve it had wide applicability for constructing buildings and laying out land.

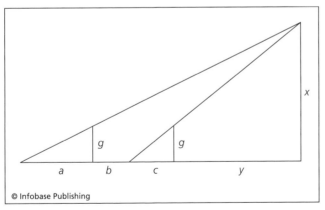

© Infobase Publishing

Āryabhata described geometrical techniques for determining distances using similar triangles and gnomons.

Tables of Sines

Āryabhata helped to promote the construction and use of sine tables, a trigonometric concept that matured in India during the

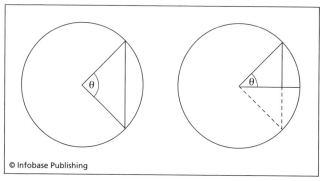

© Infobase Publishing

Rather than determining the chord associated with each angle, Āryabhata computed the half-chord of twice the angle.

fifth century. In 140 B.C.E., the Greek astronomer Hipparchus had produced a table that indicated the lengths of the chords associated with central angles in a circle of radius 3,438. Indian astronomical treatises called *siddhāntas* from the early fifth century presented a more useful table of "half-chords," called *jyā-ardha* (chord-half) or simply *jyā*. For each central angle, the table listed half the length of the chord that was cut off by a central angle twice as large in a circle of radius 3,438. This concept of *jyā*, which was translated into Arabic as *jiba* or *jaib* and then into Latin as *sinus*, became the modern sine function.

In the introduction to his book, Āryabhata gave a list of values now known as "sine differences" that could be used to calculate the sines of 24 equally spaced angles between 0° and 90°. For each angle $\theta_1 = \dfrac{90°}{24} = 3\dfrac{3}{4}°, \theta_2 = 7\dfrac{1}{2}°, \theta_3 = 11\dfrac{1}{4}°, \ldots, \theta_{24} = 90°$, the length of the associated half-chord was given by $\sin(\theta_n) = D_1 + D_2 + \ldots + D_n$ or $\sin(\theta_n) = \sin(\theta_{n-1}) + D_n$ where D_n was the nth sine difference. In addition to listing the 24 sine differences, Āryabhata provided a formula that could be used to compute their values directly. His method was equivalent to using the formula $\sin(\theta_n) = \sin(\theta_{n-1}) + \left[\sin(\theta_1) - \dfrac{\sin(\theta_1) + \cdots + \sin(\theta_{n-1})}{\sin(\theta_1)} \right]$.

He also described how to calculate the versed sine or 1 - cos(θ) for each of these 24 angles. Although the *Āryabhatīya* contained no tables or diagrams, the table of 24 angles with their associated sines, sine differences, and versed sines became known as Āryabhata's table of sines and appeared in many later treatises on mathematics and astronomy.

Algebraic Advances

In fifth-century India, the word *mathematics* meant arithmetic, geometry, and trigonometry. Āryabhata was one of a series of mathematicians who introduced algebraic techniques for solving equations. The study of the periodic nature of planetary orbits required the solution of indeterminate linear equations of the form $ax + by = c$ for integer coefficients a, b, and c. The *Āryabhatīya* contained the earliest-known record of the use of a systematic algebraic approach for solving such equations. Building on the method developed centuries earlier by the Greek mathematicians Euclid of Alexandria and Diophantus, he used the Euclidean algorithm to repeatedly replace a given linear equation by another equation having smaller coefficients. He then worked his way back from the solution of the final equation to re-create the solution of the original equation. This method of repeatedly reducing equations to other equations with smaller coefficients became known as *kuttaka*, which literally means the "pulverizer." Āryabhata focused exclusively on methods for finding the smallest positive integers that satisfied a given linear equation. In the seventh century, Brahmagupta developed this method fully to find the infinitely many solutions of each such equation.

Astronomical Theories

Āryabhata's most controversial statements were the revolutionary theories in astronomy that he stated in the *Golapāda* section of the treatise. He agreed with the prevailing ideas that the Earth was a sphere and that it stood at the center of the universe. He rejected the theory that the Earth was a motionless object around which the stars moved continuously from east to west. Instead, he proposed the radical idea that the stars were fixed in the heavens and their apparent motion resulted from the Earth's rotation on its axis. Āryabhata explained that when a human sails down a river in a boat, he or she observes that the stationary objects on the shore appear to be moving in the opposite direction. By the same principle of relative motion, as the Earth rotates from west to east on its axis, the fixed stars seem to move in the opposite direction. This theory of axial rotation was so controversial that for centuries many commentators of the *Āryabhatīya* rewrote this portion of the text to agree with the theory of a stationary Earth that religious and scientific authorities endorsed.

In connection with the rotation of the Earth, Āryabhata discussed different observers' perceptions of the stars and the Sun. He explained that a person standing at the North Pole would observe half of the stars in the sky while a person at the South Pole would see the other half of the stars. The two polar observers would also see the stars spinning in opposite directions. A person standing on the Earth's equator would see the Sun for half a day at a time. In contrast, a person at either pole would see the Sun for six months at a time while a person on the Moon would see the Sun for half a lunar month.

In his theory of the universe, Āryabhata accepted the common notion that the Sun, the Moon, and the planets orbited around the Earth. He endorsed the theory of epicyclic orbits, according to which each celestial body revolved in a small circular path as it traveled along a larger circular orbit about the Earth. He gave complicated formulas to determine each planet's location on its larger orbital path, called its mean longitude, and its periodic deviations from this path, called its true longitude.

According to Hindu religious teachings, a day in the life of the universe was determined by the passage of a fundamental number of years known as a *mahayuga* that was measured as the time it took for all the planets traveling on their different obits to align. Āryabhata gave the traditional value of 4,320,000 years for one *mahayuga*. He specified that in this time period, the Earth would rotate 1,582,237,500 times, and the Moon would complete 57,753,336 orbits of the Earth. He also specified the number of orbits completed by Mercury, Venus, Mars, Jupiter, and Saturn during each *mahayuga*. The ratios of these values gave the length of the year as 365 days, six hours, 12 minutes, and 30 seconds and the length of the sidereal (lunar) month as 27 days, nine hours, 30 minutes, and 55 seconds. Modern astronomers do not know how Āryabhata obtained numbers that produced such accurate astronomical ratios.

In the two astronomical sections of the treatise, Āryabhata correctly explained many other phenomena as well. He wrote that the Sun and the stars had their own sources of light while the Moon and the planets were illuminated by the reflected light of the Sun. Based on this idea, he explained that the disappearance of the Moon during a lunar eclipse was due to its passing into the shadow cast by the Earth as the Moon, Earth, and Sun became temporarily aligned. Likewise, he explained that an eclipse of the Sun occurred when the Moon became positioned between the Sun and the Earth casting its shadow onto the Earth. Additionally, using the values for the periods of the orbits of the Sun, the Moon, and the planets, he produced approximate calculations for the radii of each planet's orbit.

Second Astronomical Treatise

Before his death in 550, Āryabhata produced a second, more detailed treatise on mathematics and astronomy titled *Āryabhatasiddhānta* (Astronomical treatise of Āryabhata). In this work, he explained and advocated for the adoption of his *ārdharātrika* (midnight system), in which each calendar day would be measured from midnight to midnight. This system would result in each day being of uniform duration compared to the common practice of counting each day from sunrise to sunrise resulting in variable-length days. He also calculated new estimates for the distances and mean motions of the planets, revising the values he had given in his prior treatise. Other than these two innovations, researchers know little about the contents of this lost manuscript.

Conclusion

On April 19, 1975, when Indians launched the country's first satellite into orbit around the Earth, scientists and government officials honored the memory of Āryabhata by naming it after him. The deployment of the 800-pound satellite resulted from a three-year collaboration between scientists in India and the Soviet Union. Orbiting the Earth every 93 minutes, the satellite carried instruments to conduct experiments on X-ray astronomy, solar physics, and aeronomy—the study of the Earth's upper atmosphere. Although a malfunctioning transformer rendered its instruments unusable after four days, the *Āryabhata* initiated one of the world's most prolific satellite programs.

Mathematical and scientific treatises seldom remain relevant and in use for hundreds of years. The fact that Hindu scholars continued to preserve the *Āryabhatīya* for more than 10 centuries indicates the quality and the value of this masterpiece of mathematics and astronomy. Although the reverence of tradition has tended to attribute to its author a greater number of original ideas than can accurately be credited to him, it is difficult to overstate the work's central role in the preservation and development of the two disciplines in India. Āryabhata's innovations include the first alphabetical system of notation and the controversial theory of the Earth's axial rotation. In addition to these original ideas, he promoted the use of sine tables, the development of algebraic methods for solving equations, a more accurate value of π, precise ratios of planetary motion, and other advanced mathematical and astronomical ideas of his era.

FURTHER READING

Boyer, Carl B., and Uta C. Merzbach. "Chapter 12. China and India." In *A History of Mathematics*. 2nd ed. 195–224. New York: Wiley, 1991. Overview of mathematical developments in China and India.

Kramer, Jennifer. "Āryabhata the Elder." In *Notable Mathematicians from Ancient Times to the Present*, edited by Robin V. Young, 21–23. Detroit: Gale, 1998. Brief biography.

O'Connor, J. J., and E. F. Robertson. "Āryabhata the Elder." In "MacTutor History of Mathematics Archive." University of Saint Andrews. Available online. URL: http://turnbull.mcs.st-and.ac.uk/~history/Mathematicians/Aryabhata_I.html. Accessed March 25, 2005. Online biography, from the University of Saint Andrews, Scotland.

Pingree, David. "Āryabhata I." In *Dictionary of Scientific Biography*. Vol. 1, edited by Charles C. Gillispie, 308–309. New York: Scribner, 1972. Encyclopedic biography.

7

Brahmagupta

(598–668 c.e.)

Brahmagupta wrote about diverse areas of mathematics, including computations with negative numbers, cyclic quadrilaterals, and iterative approximation algorithms. Portions of the stone sextant at the Ujjain Observatory where he spent most of his professional life remain intact. *(Dinodia/ The Image Works)*

Father of Numerical Analysis

Brahmagupta (pronounced brah-mah-GOOP-tah), one of India's most famous astronomers and mathematicians, made significant contributions to astronomy, arithmetic, algebra, geometry, and numerical analysis. His two classic works on astronomy and mathematics were widely used throughout India and were instrumental in spreading the Hindu number system to the Arabic world. One of these books was the oldest-known manuscript in which negative numbers and the number zero were used in arithmetic computations. He developed sophisticated algebraic techniques for solving indeterminate linear and quadratic equations. In geometry, he produced theorems and formulas for analyzing cyclic quadrilaterals. His interpolation algorithms for estimating square roots and approximating the sines of angles established the field of numerical analysis.

Brahmagupta was born in 598 in northwestern India. The appendage "gupta" at the end of his name and the name of his father, Jisnugupta, indicate that his family may have been members of the Vaisya caste. He lived most of his life in Bhillamāla, the modern city of Bhinmal near Mount Abu in Rajasthan. In his day, this city was the capital of the kingdom ruled by the Gurjara dynasty. Indian mathematicians who commented on his writings referred to him as Bhillamālacarya, the teacher from Bhillamāla. King Vyāghramukha appointed him to the position of court astronomer. Eventually, he became the director of the astronomical observatory at Ujjain, the leading institution for mathematical and astronomical research in India at the time.

Brāhmasphutasiddhānta (Improved Astronomical System of Brāhma)

At the age of 30, Brahmagupta produced a book on astronomy and mathematics titled *Brāhmasphutasiddhānta*. The title of this work literally meant "Improved astronomical system of Brāhma," but it has also been known as "The opening of the universe." This work was one of a series of *siddhāntas* (astronomical systems) in which Indian astronomers presented rules for determining the paths and locations of heavenly bodies as well as tables of values of sines of angles. Brahmagupta wrote in the Sanskrit language, using the traditional style of poetic verse so readers would find the methods in the book easy to memorize. As previous authors had done, he incorporated the work of his predecessors, freely indicating that his book corrected and extended the information presented in the earlier work *Brāhmasiddhānta* (Astronomical system of Brahma).

The book consisted of 24 chapters, with a 25th chapter of tables appended to some translations. Brahmagupta wrote the first 10 chapters as the initial version of his book and at a later time added the second group of 14 chapters. The *Dasādhyāyī*, as the first 10 chapters are known, addressed the major issues that were of interest to astronomers. The first two chapters described the orbits of the Sun, Moon, and the known planets and gave methods for determining their mean and true longitudes. Chapter three presented methods to solve the three problems of diurnal motion—determining the location, direction of movement, and time that each heavenly body appeared on any day of the year. The next two chapters provided methods for predicting solar and lunar eclipses. Chapter six gave techniques for determining heliacal risings and settings—the appearance and disappearance of stars as they passed behind the Sun. In the next two chapters in the initial version of the book, he gave methods for predicting the phases and cycles of the Moon. The final pair of chapters provided techniques for determining planetary conjunctions when planets aligned with each other and with major stars.

In the 14 additional chapters, Brahmagupta addressed topics in both astronomy and mathematics. He reviewed previous astronomical treatises, provided additional material to supplement six of the 10 initial chapters, discussed the use of astronomical instruments, and concluded with a summary of the entire work. Four of the additional chapters and a portion of a fifth focused on mathematical issues and techniques. Chapter 12, titled *Ganita* (Mathematics), discussed topics in arithmetic and geometry. Algebraic methods for solving several classes of equations were presented in chapter 18, *Kuttaka* (Algebra). Chapter 19, *Sanku-chaya-vijnana* (On the gnomon), described trigonometric methods for determining distances using vertical poles called gnomons. Additional techniques for measuring were presented in chapter 20, *Chandas-citi-uttara* (On meters). Seven stanzas of chapter 21, *Gola* (Spheres), discussed measurements of arcs and other topics in spherical trigonometry.

In addition to collecting the theories, knowledge, and techniques that generations of Indian astronomers had accumulated, Brahmagupta presented several ideas that further advanced the state of the science. Although he accepted the conventional (but flawed) theory that the Earth was the center of the universe, with the Sun, Moon, and planets orbiting around it, he provided his improved estimate for the size of the spherical Earth, calculating its circumference as 5,000 *yojanas* (ca. 22,500 miles, or 36,000 km). He also presented his calculation for the length of a year as 365 days, six hours, five minutes, and 19 seconds, an estimate that differed by less than four minutes from the actual length of a sidereal year—the time it takes for the Earth to complete one revolution of its orbit. Brahmagupta made frequent use of algebraic techniques to solve equations that arose in astronomy. This contrasted with earlier works that made limited use of algebra, relying more heavily on arithmetic and geometric methods.

Astronomers throughout India studied the *Brāhmasphutasiddhānta* extensively and for two centuries considered it to be the authoritative astronomical work. In the late eighth century, Islamic scholars translated it into Arabic and gave it the title *Zīj al-sindhind* (Astronomical tables of India). The work remained known to the Western world only through this version until 1817, when Henry T. Colebrooke provided the first English translation of the original Sanskrit edition.

Arithmetical Innovations

The four-and-a-half chapters of the *Brāhmasphutasiddhānta* that were devoted to mathematics were densely packed with a rich variety of results and techniques. As he did in the portions of the book that dealt with astronomy, Brahmagupta mixed several of his original ideas and methods with the classic results of his mathematical predecessors.

In Chapter 12, titled *Ganita*, Brahmagupta gave rules for performing arithmetic with "fortunes" (positive numbers), "debts" (negative numbers), and *sunya* (zero). He defined zero as the result obtained by subtracting any number from itself. His rules stated that when zero was added to or subtracted from any number, the number remained unchanged, and that any number multiplied by zero became zero. He gave rules indicating that the product of two negative numbers was a positive number and that a negative number subtracted from zero produced a positive result. Although historians do not credit Brahmagupta with inventing the concepts of zero and negative numbers, his *Brāhmasphutasiddhānta* was a landmark achievement, as it was the oldest-known mathematical work in which zero and negative numbers appeared in arithmetical operations.

Brahmagupta attempted to extend the rules of arithmetic to address division by zero, making the distinction that zero divided by zero was zero, while any other number divided by zero was a fraction with zero in the denominator. The proper interpretation of these incorrect rules was not provided until the 12th century, when Indian mathematician Bhāskara II introduced the concept of infinity. Despite these errors, mathematicians consider Brahmagupta's rules for arithmetic with zeros and negative numbers to be a significant milestone in the development of the theory of arithmetic.

In the same chapter, Brahmagupta explained many techniques used to perform arithmetic computations. He gave four methods for *gomutrika*, the multiplication of numbers having multiple digits such as $342 \cdot 617$. All four methods were similar to the modern pencil-and-paper technique, differing primarily in the location where the digits of the second factor were written in order to produce the intermediate results. He also provided classic formulas for summing the series $1 + 2 + 3 + \ldots + n$, $1^2 + 2^2 + 3^2 + \ldots + n^2$, and $1^3 + 2^3 + 3^3 + \ldots + n^3$ correctly, giving their results as

$$\frac{n(n+1)}{2}, \quad \frac{n(n+1)(2n+1)}{6}, \text{ and } \left[\frac{n(n+1)}{2}\right]^2,$$

respectively. Working with fractions, he explained how to solve proportions using the "rule of three" and how to reduce compound fractions to simple fractions. Brahmagupta included problems about compound interest and other applications to illustrate various computational techniques.

When Islamic scholars translated the *Brāhmasphutasiddhānta* into Arabic in the late eighth century, the arithmetic portion of the manuscript so persuasively demonstrated the computational superiority of the Hindu's base-10 number system that they adopted it throughout the Arabic empire. They renamed the numeral *sunya* as *zifr*, which European mathematicians translated into Latin as *zephirum* and later into English as "cipher" or "zero." Arabic mathematicians did not, however, embrace the concept of negative numbers. The fact that European mathematicians did not develop a thorough understanding of negative numbers until the 16th century indicates the advanced state of mathematics that

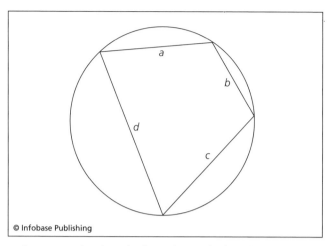

Brahmagupta developed a formula to calculate the area of a cyclic quadrilateral.

Brahmagupta and his contemporaries had attained in the early seventh century.

New Geometrical Techniques

In addition to explaining the rules and techniques of arithmetic, Brahmagupta included material about geometry. He presented three new results about cyclic quadrilaterals—four-sided figures whose vertices were four points on a circle. He gave a formula (which has come to be known as Brahmagupta's formula) for calculating the area of such a figure. If the lengths of the sides were

a, b, c, and d and $s = \frac{1}{2}(a + b + c + d)$ represented the semi-perimeter,

then the area of the cyclic quadrilateral was given by

$A = \sqrt{(s - a)(s - b)(s - c)(s - d)}$. This formula generalized the similar

formula for calculating the area of a triangle discovered in the first century by the Greek mathematician Heron of Alexandria.

Brahmagupta also presented formulas to calculate the lengths of the two diagonals of a cyclic quadrilateral. One diagonal had

length $l_1 = \sqrt{\dfrac{(ab + cd)(ac + bd)}{(ad + bc)}}$ while the other had length

$l_2 = \sqrt{\dfrac{(ad + bc)(ac + bd)}{(ab + cd)}}$. He illustrated the formulas for the area and the lengths of the diagonals by providing an example of a cyclic quadrilateral with sides of lengths $a = 52$, $b = 25$, $c = 39$, and $d = 60$. The area of this figure was 1,764, and the lengths of its diagonals were and $l_1 = 56$ and $l_2 = 63$.

He also stated a rule, now known as Brahmagupta's theorem, that applied to cyclic quadrilaterals whose diagonals were perpendicular to each other. The theorem stated:

> In cyclic quadrilateral $ABCD$, if $\overline{AC}$ is perpendicular to $\overline{BD}$ at point E, then the perpendicular from E to $\overline{AB}$ will bisect the opposite side $\overline{CD}$.

As he did with all the techniques in his book, Brahmagupta stated this theorem without proving why it was valid. A straightforward proof can be constructed by showing that, in the diagram below, angles 1, 2, 3, and 4 are equal and that angles 5, 6, 7, and 8 are equal.

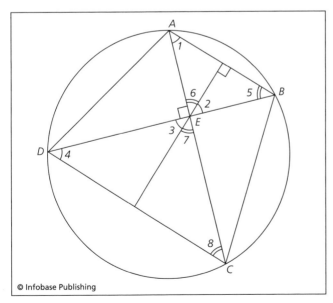

© Infobase Publishing

Brahmagupta's theorem deals with cyclic quadrilaterals whose diagonals are perpendicular.

Most historians theorize that Brahmagupta probably had constructed proofs of his theoretical results and that he likely taught them to his students and his contemporaries. They further believe that the *Brāhmasphutasiddhānta* constituted only a brief summary of these results and techniques presented in a lyric form to make them easy to recall. Other historians dissent from this position, suggesting that Brahmagupta and other mathematicians of his era may have accepted theorems and formulas after having verified them with a large number of examples.

Algebraic Methods

In chapter 18, titled *Kuttaka*, Brahmagupta presented advanced algebraic techniques to solve four types of equations. The literal translation of *kuttaka* as "pulverizer" accurately conveyed the power and effectiveness of the methods he employed. Using the first letters from the names of the colors for red, green, and blue, Brahmagupta described a procedure for determining one of the roots of a second-degree equation. Using modern algebraic notation, his technique gave $x = \dfrac{\sqrt{4ac + b^2} - b}{2a}$ as a root of the equation $ax^2 + bx = c$.

This result coincided with one of the two roots produced by the modern quadratic formula. In solving such equations, he recognized negative and irrational quantities as valid solutions.

Brahmagupta presented the first systematic procedure to determine the general solution of linear equations of the form $ax + c = by$, where a, b, and c were integer coefficients. These indeterminate equations having infinitely many integer solutions arose in astronomical problems where an event occurred a certain number of days into one celestial cycle (such as the orbit of a planet) and a different number of days after some other recurring astronomical event. Astronomers reduced the problem of finding a number N that satisfied two linear congruences, such as $N = ax + d$ and $N = by + e$ for known integer values a, b, d, and e, to solving a single equation $ax + c = by$. Employing the methods first developed by the ancient Greek mathematicians Euclid and Diophantus and later enhanced by the fifth-century Indian Āryabhata, he used the

Euclidean algorithm to find the greatest common divisor of a and b. He then combined intermediate results obtained in that process to find a solution of the original equation. Extending the work of his predecessors, Brahmagupta showed that if $x = p$, $y = q$ was a solution of the equation, then, as m ranged over the entire set of integers, the formulas $x = p + mb$, $y = q + ma$ produced the complete set of solutions. He illustrated his method by using the solution $x = 10$, $y = 23$ of the equation $137x + 10 = 60y$ to generate other solutions, including $x = 10 + 60 = 70$, $y = 23 + 137 = 160$ and $x = 10 + 2 \cdot 60 = 130$, $y = 23 + 2 \cdot 137 = 297$. As he solved these indeterminate linear equations and investigated their astronomical origins, Brahmagupta theorized that all the planets would be aligned once every 4,320,000,000 years. Some Hindu astronomers believed that after this *kalpa*, or fundamental period of the universe, earthly events, like their celestial counterparts, would reoccur.

The algebraic chapter also presented Brahmagupta's solutions to a second class of indeterminate equations, quadratic equations of the form $ax^2 \pm c = y^2$ for integer coefficients a and c. Although he did not fully develop the general method of solution, Brahmagupta explained a procedure that obtained infinitely many solutions for each example that he presented. He challenged his contemporaries to find the smallest integer solution of the equation $92x^2 + 1 = y^2$, asserting that anyone who could solve this problem within a year deserved to be called a mathematician. After setting this challenge, he explained his method of solution by starting with an obvious solution $x = 1$, $y = 10$ for the related equation $92x^2 + 8 = y^2$ and showing how to develop efficiently this result into the desired answer $x = 120$, $y = 1{,}151$. In addition to this particular example, known as Brahmagupta's equation, he demonstrated the wide applicability of his method for solving equations ranging from $11x^2 + 1 = y^2$ that had the simple solution $x = 3$, $y = 10$ to equations like $61x^2 + 1 = y^2$ whose smallest solution was $x = 226{,}153{,}980$, $y = 1{,}766{,}319{,}049$. Equations of this form have become known as Pell's equation, after the 17th-century mathematician John Pell, even though the 11th-century Indian mathematician Acarya Jayadeva had provided a complete solution for all cases 600 years earlier.

From his method for solving indeterminate quadratic equations, Brahmagupta developed a technique for estimating square roots.

To find the square root of the positive integer N, he used the solution of the equation $Nx^2 + 1 = y^2$ to start an iterative process of successive approximations yielding $\sqrt{N} \approx \dfrac{y_i}{x_i}$, where $x_i = 2x_{i-1}y_{i-1}$ and $y_i = y^2_{i-1} + Nx^2_{i-1}$. This sophisticated technique was equivalent to the Newton-Raphson method developed by Sir Isaac Newton and first published by Joseph Raphson in 1690. Their method gave the series of estimates $z_i = z_{i-1} - \dfrac{z^2_{i-1} - N}{2z_{i-1}}$ or, more simply, $z_i = \dfrac{z_{i-1}}{2} + \dfrac{N}{2z_{i-1}}$.

The other mathematical sections of the *Brāhmasphutasiddhānta* presented additional ideas of significance. In several places, Brahmagupta used the estimate $\pi \approx \sqrt{10}$, a value that had appeared in earlier Indian manuscripts. He showed that the product of two numbers, each of which was a sum of two squares, was itself a sum of two squares. The equation that he described, known as Brahmagupta's identity, $(a^2 + b^2)\cdot(c^2 + d^2) = (ac - bd)^2 + (ad + bc)^2$, demonstrated his facility with algebraic manipulations. He also gave the first-known description of a perpetual motion machine. His design involved a wheel whose hollow spokes were half-filled with mercury. The design relied on the incorrect belief that the

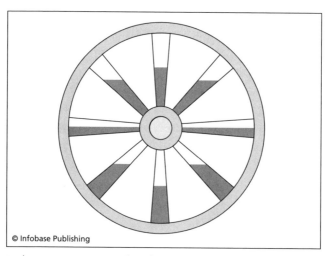

Brahmagupta attempted to design a perpetual motion machine by half-filling the hollow spokes of a wheel with mercury.

mercury would run up the sides in some spokes and down in others, causing the wheel to rotate forever.

Second Astronomical Treatise

In 665, at the age of 67, Brahmagupta produced a second book on astronomy and mathematics titled *Khandakhādyaka*. This *karana* (astronomical handbook) contained brief formulations rather than the fuller development of geometrical models and theories of cosmology typically found in *siddhāntas* (astronomical systems) such as his earlier work. The first eight chapters, known as the *Purva-khandakhādyaka*, summarized the teachings of Āryabhata with few alterations or additions. They constituted a more concise presentation of many of the same topics addressed in the first 10 chapters of the *Brāhmasphutasiddhānta*, including solar and lunar eclipses; planetary risings, settings, and conjunctions; the size and orientation of the Moon's crescent; and the location of major stars and constellations. One of the changes he made was to include a revised estimate for the length of the year as 365 days, six hours, 12 minutes, and 36 seconds, which overestimated the true length of a sidereal year by less than four minutes.

Brahmagupta supplemented this summary with an appendix titled *Uttara-khandakhādyaka*. He reproduced Āryabhata's table of sines, which gave the sines of 24 angles between $3\frac{3}{4}^\circ$ and $90°$ measured in increments of $3\frac{3}{4}^\circ$ and the corresponding intermediate values known as "sine differences." Brahmagupta then provided a new interpolation formula to compute the sine of any angle not listed in the table. Representing the angle as $x_i + \theta$, where x_i was one of the listed angles and θ was an increment smaller than $3\frac{3}{4}^\circ$, he estimated its sine using the formula

$$\sin(x_i + \theta) \approx \sin(x_i) + \frac{\theta}{2\left(3\frac{3}{4}\right)}(D_i + D_{i+1}) - \frac{\theta^2}{2\left(3\frac{3}{4}\right)^2}(D_i - D_{i+1}), \text{ where}$$

D_i was the ith sine difference. Dividing this result by 3,438, the radius of the circle used as the basis for the computations, produced values very close to those generated by the modern trigonometric sine function. This accurate and intricate formula is a special case of the more general Newton-Stirling interpolation formula developed in the 18th century by Sir Isaac Newton and Scottish mathematician James Stirling. This formula and his method of successive approximations for square roots marked the beginning of numerical analysis, the branch of mathematics concerned with iterative algorithms used to approximate the solutions of equations or the values of functions. As the creator of the earliest-known iterative approximation algorithms, Brahmagupta earned the title "Father of Numerical Analysis."

In addition to this interpolation formula to approximate the sine of an angle, Brahmagupta presented an algebraic formula that gave a different estimate. He obtained the formula

$\sin(\varphi) \approx \dfrac{4\varphi(180-\varphi)}{40,500 - \varphi(180-\varphi)} \cdot 3,438$ from the work of his contem-

porary, the Indian astronomer Bhāskara I. Although it was less accurate than his "double difference formula," it was easier to calculate and provided reasonably accurate estimates.

Brahmagupta died in 668 at the age of 70, three years after writing the *Khandakhādyaka*. Five centuries later, India's greatest astronomer-mathematician, Bhāskara II, paid tribute to the man who greatly influenced his work, giving him the title *Ganita Chakra Chudamani*, meaning the "gem of the circle of mathematicians."

Conclusion

Through his teachings and his two books, *Brāhmasphutasiddhānta* and *Khandakhādyaka*, Brahmagupta advanced the knowledge of mathematics and astronomy in his country. For five centuries after his death, his Indian successors further developed his ideas about arithmetic with zero and negative numbers, his methods for solving indeterminate linear and quadratic equations, his geometrical results about cyclic quadrilaterals, and his approximation techniques for trigonometric functions. Beyond the borders of his own country, his major influence on the development of mathematics was the demonstration of the advantages of the Hindu system of numbers. Through the Arabic translations of his works and the Latin translations of the works of Arabic scholars that were derived from his books, the European mathematical community eventually adopted this numbering system. Many centuries after his death, European mathematicians rediscovered independently most of his techniques, formulas, and theories. He remained largely unknown to the Western world until Colebrooke's 19th-century translation of his *Brāhmasphutasiddhānta*.

FURTHER READING

Boyer, Carl B., and Uta C. Merzbach. "Chapter 12. China and India." In *A History of Mathematics*. 2nd ed. 195–224. Overview of mathematical developments in China and India.

O'Connor, J. J., and E. F. Robertson. "Brahmagupta." In "MacTutor History of Mathematics Archive." University of Saint Andrews. Available online. URL: http://turnbull.mcs.st-and .ac.uk/~history/Mathematicians/Brahmagupta.html. Accessed March 25, 2005. Online biography, from the University of Saint Andrews, Scotland.

Pingree, David. "Brahmagupta." In *Dictionary of Scientific Biography*. Vol. 2, edited by Charles C. Gillispie, 416–418. New York: Scribner, 1972. Encyclopedic biography.

Weisstein, Eric W. "MathWorld." Available online. URL: http:// mathworld.wolfram.com. Accessed March 25, 2005. Seven articles about Brahmagupta's mathematics, including Brahmagupta's theorem and Brahmagupta's equation.

8
Abū Ja'far Muhammad ibn Mūsā al-Khwārizmī

(ca. 800–ca. 847 C.E.)

Muhammad al-Khwārizmī's treatise about solving second-degree equations initiated the formal study of algebra. (*Sovphoto/Eastphoto*)

Father of Algebra

Abū Ja'far Muhammad ibn Mūsā al-Khwārizmī (pronounced al-hwa-RIZ-mee) was the most prominent mathematician at Baghdad's House of Wisdom. His pioneering work demonstrating how to solve second-degree equations introduced the formal subject of algebra. His book explaining how to use the Hindu's base-10 number system was so influential that this system of arithmetic came to be known as Arabic numerals, and the method of computation was called algorithm, after the Latin translation of his name. As an applied scientist, he created an improved set of astronomical tables and a more accurate geographical atlas of the world. He also wrote a variety of scholarly treatises on such diverse topics as the Jewish calendar, the construction and operation of the astrolabe, the use of sundials, and a political history of his era. His two main mathematical works were widely translated throughout Europe and influenced the development of mathematics for eight centuries.

Early Years

Al-Khwārizmī's full name indicates that he was Muhammad, father of Ja'far and son of Mūsā (or Moses). The name al-Khwārizmī meant that his family came from Khwārizm, a region of central Asia, although historians generally agree that he was born, or at least raised, near Baghdad in present-day Iraq. He was born before 800 and died after 847, but no specific dates are available to mark either end of his life.

Caliph al-Ma'mūn, ruler of the Islamic empire from 813 to 833, invited al-Khwārizmī to become a member of Baghdad's Dār al-Hikma (House of Wisdom). At this center of learning, leading scholars created Arabic translations of classic works by Greek and Hindu philosophers, mathematicians, and scientists. They also engaged in substantial projects to advance the state of knowledge in mathematics, astronomy, and the sciences. In this intellectual environment, al-Khwārizmī created significant works in algebra, arithmetic, astronomy, and geography as well as several minor works on calendars, astrolabes, sundials, and history. Most of his projects cannot be accurately dated.

Text on Algebra

Al-Khwārizmī's greatest work was the mathematics book *al-Kitāb al-mukhtasar fī hisāb al-jabr wa'l-muqābala* (The compendious book on calculation by completion and balancing). The term *al-jabr*, meaning "completion" or "restoration," referred to the technique of adding the same quantity to both sides of an equation, usually to restore an amount that had been subtracted from one side of the equation. The term *al-muqābala*, meaning "balancing," described the process of subtracting a quantity from both sides of an equation, usually when the same type of term appeared on both sides of the equation. In his book, al-Khwārizmī completed the equation $x^2 = 40x - 4x^2$ by adding $4x^2$ to both sides, producing the simpler equation $5x^2 = 40x$. He balanced similarly the equation $50 + x^2 = 29 + 10x$ by subtracting 29 from both sides to produce the equivalent equation $21 + x^2 = 10x$.

The book was organized into three parts, each addressing an area of elementary practical mathematics. After some introductory remarks about the Hindu system of numbers, the first and most well-known section provided algebraic techniques for solving first- and second-degree equations. In the second part of the book, al-Khwārizmī presented geometrical methods for determining the lengths of sides of polygons, the areas of circles and other two-dimensional figures, and the volumes of spheres, cones, pyramids, and other three-dimensional objects. He then explained how to use these concepts in practical projects such as land measurement and the construction of canals. The third and longest section of the book dealt with the arithmetic needed to settle inheritances, legacies, lawsuits, partnerships, and common business transactions.

Throughout the entire book, al-Khwārizmī followed the Greek tradition of explaining mathematical manipulations in words rather than in symbols. In linear equations, he used the word *shay'*, meaning "thing," to represent an unknown quantity and *dirham*, a unit of coinage, to represent one unit of measure. In second-degree equations, he used *māl*, meaning "wealth" or "property," to represent the square of the unknown quantity and *jidhr* meaning "root" for the unknown quantity itself.

Using this rhetorical technique, al-Khwārizmī identified six standard forms of equations that could be used to represent and solve every application presented in the book. In modern algebraic notation with the variable x and with positive integer coefficients a, b, and c, these forms were one type of linear or first-degree equation

1. $bx = c$

and five types of quadratic or second-degree equations

2. $ax^2 = bx$
3. $ax^2 = c$
4. $ax^2 + bx = c$
5. $ax^2 + c = bx$
6. $ax^2 = bx + c$

In modern notation, all six forms of equations can be generalized as $ax^2 + bx + c = 0$, where the coefficients a, b, and c are positive, negative, or zero. Al-Khwārizmī classified these equations into six forms because he did not recognize the existence of negative numbers or the use of zero as a coefficient, concepts that were not widely used in the mathematical community until eight centuries later.

As an indication of the complexity required in al-Khwārizmī's explanations, his solution to equations of type (6) $ax^2 = bx + c$ translates

into modern algebraic notation as $x = \sqrt{\left(\frac{1}{2}\left(\frac{b}{a}\right)\right)^2 + \left(\frac{c}{a}\right)} + \left(\frac{1}{2}\right)\left(\frac{b}{a}\right)$.

Through a number of examples, he explained how to use the techniques of *al-jabr* and *al-muqābala* to reduce any other equation involving roots and squares to one of these six forms.

Al-Khwārizmī used a geometric version of the algebraic technique known as completing the square to solve forms of quadratic equations that involved three terms. To solve the example $x^2 + 10x = 39$, he drew a square with each side having length x. He then attached a rectangle of width $\frac{5}{2}$ and length x to each side of the square. The combined area of this square and the four attached rectangles was $x^2 + 4\left(\frac{5}{2}x\right) = x^2 + 10x$, a quantity that equaled 39 in the given equation. He then showed that filling in the four corners, each of which was a square measuring 5/2 on each side added

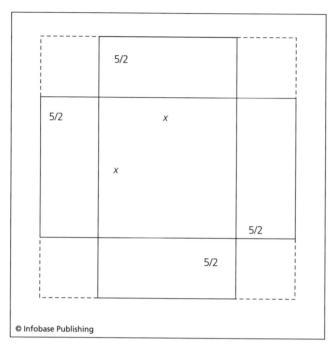

Al-Khwārizmī used a geometrical version of the completing the square technique to solve the equation $x^2 + 10x = 39$.

$4\left(\dfrac{5}{2}\right)\left(\dfrac{5}{2}\right)$ = 25 square units of area to the figure. The resulting square had sides of length $x + 5$ and total area of $39 + 25 = 64$. He concluded his solution by reasoning that the area of the large square was $(x + 5)^2 = 8^2$. Ignoring negative numbers, the solution would have to be $x + 5 = 8$, so $x = 3$.

The algebraic portion of the book concluded with a brief section titled "On Business Transactions," in which al-Khwārizmī explained the "rule of three." In this type of problem, a merchant or customer determined the price of a certain quantity of merchandise given the price of a different quantity of the same item by using equivalent ratios. He also solved examples of a slight variation of this problem in which two prices and one quantity were given, and one needed to determine the desired quantity that would balance the equation.

In creating this mathematical work, al-Khwārizmī drew heavily on similar works by Greek, Hindu, and Hebrew mathematicians. Although much of his material and some of his methods were more elementary than similar material in many of these classic works, the completeness of his method for solving quadratic equations and the usefulness of his general *al-jabr* and *al-muqābala* techniques earned the book immediate acceptance and recognition. Arabic mathematicians adopted his techniques for manipulating and solving equations and used his book as a standard mathematics text for several centuries.

The Latin translations of al-Khwārizmī's book, provided in the 12th century by English mathematician Robert of Chester and Italian mathematician Gherard of Cremona, introduced his algebraic techniques to Europe. His use of the rhetorical form—including the terms *shay'* and *māl* that translated into Latin as *cossa* and *census*, respectively—became standard algebraic techniques until the 16th century, when François Viète popularized the symbolic form of algebra using letters for variables and coefficients. His book exerted such a dominant influence on medieval European mathematics that the name for the branch of mathematics known as algebra was derived from the term *al-jabr* in the title of his book. Because his book was the first to teach algebra as a separate branch of mathematics, he is credited as being the "Father of Algebra."

Text on Arithmetic

Al-Khwārizmī wrote a second mathematics book on the use of Hindu numerals. The original Arabic manuscript no longer exists, but this important work is well known through its Latin translation *Algoritmi de numero Indorum* (al-Khwārizmī on the Hindu art of reckoning). Its original title is not known for certain, but translators have suggested *Kitāb al-jam' wa'l-tafrīq bi hisāb al-hind* (Book of addition and subtraction by the method of the Hindus) or *Kitāb hisāb al-'adad al-hindī* (Treatise on calculation with the Hindu numerals) as possible titles of his original Arabic work. The book introduced the base-10 number system that the Arabs had learned from the Hindus of India, in which the numerals 1 through 9 and the symbol 0 were used to represent any positive integer quantity.

In this place-value numbering system, the same symbol could be used to represent a particular number of units or that many groups of 10, 100, or any power of 10. For example, in the number 7,267, the leftmost "7" represents 7,000, while the rightmost "7" represents seven individual units.

After showing how values were represented with these Hindu numerals, al-Khwārizmī discussed how to perform a variety of straightforward arithmetic computations beginning with simple addition, subtraction, multiplication, and division of integer quantities. He explained how to perform these four arithmetic operations with fractions and with mixed numbers. Since sexagesimal, or base-60 fractions, such as $23 + \dfrac{7}{60} + \dfrac{4}{60^2}$ were commonly used for astronomical computations, al-Khwārizmī explained how the Hindus wrote and calculated with them as well. He described processes for estimating square roots and cube roots. To verify the accuracy of arithmetic computations, he detailed the method of casting out nines. He also showed how the methods of false position and double false position could be used to provide purely arithmetic solutions to algebraic problems. Throughout the book, he used the numerous techniques to solve a variety of practical applications.

The mathematical content of this work was not al-Khwārizmī's original creation; his contributions were the clear and thorough explanations of how the most common and useful arithmetic computations could be performed using this numbering system. As the first Arabic work to explain systematically and persuasively the benefits of using Hindu numerals, his book was of seminal importance. Through this book's influence, Hindu numerals became widely used throughout the Islamic empire. The 12th-century Latin translations of this work inspired many European mathematicians, including John of Seville, John of Sacrobosco, and Leonardo Fibonacci, to write their own treatises espousing this system of numeration and computation. These and later works convinced the European mathematical and commercial communities to replace the use of Roman numerals by this superior number system. Al-Khwārizmī's name became so closely associated with the use of Hindu numerals that Europeans started calling them Arabic numerals, and the word *algorithm*, derived from the Latin form of his name, came to mean any method of calculating with these numerals. Eventually, algorithm came to mean any systematic, although not necessarily arithmetic, technique for solving a problem.

Astronomical Tables

In conjunction with the House of Wisdom, Caliph al-Ma'mūn established an observatory in Baghdad where al-Khwārizmī worked with a group of other astronomers on a series of projects. They tracked the path of the Sun throughout the year and accurately measured the obliquity of the ecliptic as 23° 33', a more accurate angle than the commonly accepted value of 23° 51' obtained by the Greek astronomer Theon of Alexandria in the fourth century. Through careful celestial observations, the Baghdad astronomers were able to determine more accurate coordinates for the latitudes and longitudes of many cities throughout the Islamic empire. They used these coordinates to create a detailed map of the known world using a stereographic projection centered at a point on the equator.

Al-Khwārizmī's most significant astronomical achievement was the creation of an extensive set of tables known as *Zīj al-sindhind* (Astronomical tables of India). He based much of this work on similar tables that Indian astronomer Brahmagupta had included in his seventh-century work *Brāhmasphutasiddhānta* (Improved system of Brāhma), a work that Arabic translators had named *Zīj al-sindhind*, combining the words *sind*, a region of Pakistan, and *hind*, the Arabic word for India. He also borrowed material from the massive second-century work *Almagest* (The greatest compilation), created by the Greek astronomer Claudius Ptolemy, and the more recent sixth-century work *Zīj al-shāh* (The shah's astronomical tables) compiled by the Arabic astronomer Pahlavi. For each of the seven heavenly bodies—the Sun, the Moon, Mercury, Venus, Mars, Saturn, and Jupiter—al-Khwārizmī provided a table of mean motion and a table of equations. He explained how to use this information to calculate the position and path of each body on any day of the year as well as its mean position at epoch, the position of the apogee, and the position of the node. Other tables provided the information needed to compute eclipses, solar declination, parallax, right ascension, and the phases of the Moon. To enable astronomers to perform the necessary calculations, he provided detailed trigonometric tables giving the values of the sines and tangents of angles measured in increments of 1/150th of a degree. The work also included astrological tables and material on spherical trigonometry.

These tables are the oldest Arabic astronomical work that has survived largely intact. Although many Arabic astronomers produced improved tables during the next three centuries, al-Khwārizmī's work remained a standard in Islamic classrooms. In the 12th century, Gerard of Cremona produced a Latin translation of the *Toledan Tables,* a collection of astronomical tables drawn from the work of al-Khwārizmī and other Arabic astronomers. Throughout Europe, astronomers widely used this collection of tables for 100 years.

Geographical Work

In the related area of geography, al-Khwārizmī created a major work titled *Kitāb sūrat al-ard* (Book of the form of the Earth). In tabular format, this massive book listed the latitudes and longitudes of 2,400 cities, mountains, seas, islands, regions, and rivers. Their locations were grouped into seven *climata*—horizontal strips that stretched from the Atlantic Ocean east to the Pacific Ocean. The work represented an improvement over Ptolemy's second-century *Geography,* which provided a description of a world map with a list of the coordinates of major cities and geographical features. Al-Khwārizmī's work used Ptolemy's coordinates for European features and his own more accurate observations for the coordinates of locations throughout the Islamic empire. The book incorporated the given information into several maps of different regions of the known world.

Al-Khwārizmī's geographical work was extensively used throughout the Islamic world for several centuries. As astronomers obtained more accurate information, they updated the coordinates and produced improved versions that maintained the same organizational structure. Medieval European astronomical tables incorporated his coordinates for Islamic cities and geographical features, but the entirety of his work was not fully translated until the late 19th century.

Minor Works

In addition to his major works in mathematics, astronomy, and geography, al-Khwārizmī produced several minor published works. These were less widely used, did not advance knowledge in their discipline in significant ways, and were not improved upon by later scholars. Each was an accurate, well-written treatise on a specialized subject, but none had the impact of his major works. Collectively, his entire body of work demonstrated the breadth of his knowledge and his ability to write authoritatively on a variety of subjects.

The only one of the minor works to survive in its entirety was *Istikhrāj taʾrīkh al-yahūd* (Extraction of the Jewish era). In this book, al-Khwārizmī described the Jewish calendar, which was based on a cycle of 19 years. He explained the rules used for determining variable dates within this system and how to convert dates between the Jewish system of measuring years and the Roman and Islamic systems. The work also included rules for determining the positions of the Sun and Moon on any date in the Jewish calendar.

As a practical scientist, al-Khwārizmī wrote two books about the astrolabe, an instrument invented by the Greeks to determine one's position on the sea by measuring the angles between the horizon and the stars. His two works were titled *Kitāb ʿamal al-asturlāb* (Book on the construction of the astrolabe) and *Kitāb al-ʿamal biʾl-asturlāb* (Book on the operation of the astrolabe). The first manuscript has disappeared completely; a small portion of the second book has survived. The two works were likely based on earlier Greek and Arabic treatises and were superseded by later Arabic works. As astronomers improved on the design of the astrolabe in the next two centuries, these manuals became obsolete.

Another short work produced by al-Khwārizmī was the *Kitāb al-taʾrīkh* (Chronicle of the era). This political history profiled the lives of prominent figures of his day. In this work, he used his knowledge of astronomy to explain how the significant events in their lives were consequences of their personal horoscopes.

The other works al-Khwārizmī produced no longer exist and are known only through references made by other writers. He wrote a book about sundials titled *Kitāb al-rukhāma* (Book on the sundial), but nothing is known of its contents. Portions of an Arabic manuscript on spherical trigonometry have been attributed to him, but the connection is not certain. He may have written a work on clocks, but references to this are vague and not reliable.

Conclusion

Al-Khwārizmī was the first prominent Arabic mathematician and astronomer. His works on algebra, arithmetic, astronomy, and geography brought together and improved upon the achievements of Greek and Hindu scholars. Throughout the Islamic empire, each of these four works was regarded as the authoritative treatment on the subject and was used for hundreds of years. When his two mathematics books were translated into Latin in the 12th century, they significantly influenced the development of European mathematics. They ultimately led to the adoption of the Hindu-Arabic system of numerals and to the establishment of algebra as a separate branch of mathematics. His organization and advancement of mathematics and astronomy had a lasting impact on both disciplines.

FURTHER READING

Cavette, Chris. "al-Khwārizmī' (also known as Alchorizmi and Algorismus)." In *Notable Mathematicians from Ancient Times to the Present*, edited by Robin V. Young, 274–276. Detroit: Gale, 1998. Brief biography.

Katz, Victor J. "Chapter 7. The Mathematics of Islam." In *A History of Mathematics: An Introduction.* 2nd ed. 238–287. Reading, Mass.: Addison Wesley Longmann, 1998. Chapter from college textbook explains some of al-Khwārizmī's mathematical works and provides brief biographical sketch.

O'Connor, J. J., and E. F. Robertson. "Abu Ja'far Muhammad ibn Musa al-Khwārizmī." In "MacTutor History of Mathematics

Archive." University of Saint Andrews. Available online. URL: http://turnbull.mcs.st-and.ac.uk/~history/Mathematicians/Al-Khwarizmi.html. Accessed March 25, 2005. Online biography, from the University of Saint Andrews, Scotland.

Toomer, G. J. "al-Khwārizmī, Abū Ja'far Muhammad ibn Mūsā." In *Dictionary of Scientific Biography*. Vol. 7, edited by Charles C. Gillispie, 358–365. New York: Scribner, 1972. Detailed encyclopedic biography.

9

Omar Khayyám

(ca. 1048–ca. 1131 C.E.)

Omar Khayyám developed geometrical solutions for solving algebraic equations, devised an improved calendar system, studied astronomy, and wrote poetry. (Corbis)

Mathematician, Astronomer, Philosopher, and Poet

Omar Khayyám (pronounced high-YAM) is well known in the Western world as the Persian poet who authored the collection of poems known as the *Rubáiyát*. But during his lifetime he earned greater recognition in his country for his achievements in mathematics and astronomy. In one of his four mathematics books, he identified 14 classes of cubic equations and explained geometrical techniques for solving them. He also developed a method that used binomial coefficients to approximate the nth root of an integer. While attempting to improve on Euclid's parallel postulate, Khayyám proved a set of theorems that represent the earliest-known investigations into non-Euclidean geometry. His writings about ratios unified the theories that had been developed by Greek and Arabic mathematicians. In addition to his poetry and mathematics, he wrote books on the theory of music, existential philosophy, and astronomy and created a calendar that measured the length of a year more accurately than any other calendar of his day.

Early Years

Omar Khayyám's full name was Ghiyāth al-Dīn Abū'l-Fath 'Umar ibn Ibrāhīm al-Nīshābūri al-Khayyāmī. Ghiyāth al-Dīn, meaning "the help of the faith," was an honorary title given to him later in life. 'Umar, sometimes translated as Omar, was his proper name. Ibn Ibrāhīm indicated that he was the son of Ibrāhīm. Al-Nīshābūri identified the city of Nīshābūr, the provincial capital of Khurasan (modern-day Iran), as his birthplace. Al-Khayyāmī indicated that his father earned his living as a tentmaker.

The date of Khayyám's birth is less certain. Abu'l-Hasan al-Bayhaqī, a Persian historian who knew Khayyám, created a detailed personal horoscope for him using May 15, 1048, as the date of his birth. Most historical sources are less specific, placing his date of birth between 1038 and 1048. Some sources claim that he was born as early as 1017 or 1023.

As a young man, Khayyám studied the Koran and Muslim traditions in Nīshābūr as a student of Imám Mowaffak, a revered wise man from Khurasan. At this school, he became friends with Nizām al-Mulk, whose father was sultan Toghrul Beg the Tartar, the ruler of Persia and founder of the Seljukian dynasty. After these years of study, Khayyám acquired an extensive knowledge of philosophy, mathematics, and science and earned his living as a private tutor in the courts of wealthy magistrates.

When al-Mulk became a vizier, administering governmental affairs during the reign of Sultan Alp Arslan, he persuaded the sultan to grant Khayyám a yearly pension of 1,200 *mithkáls* of gold. This stipend enabled Khayyám to undertake independent investigations of new ideas in mathematics and science. During this period of years, he wrote three books, each of which presented original theories.

Early Writings on Arithmetic, Algebra, and Music

Khayyám's earliest work was an arithmetic book titled *Mushkilāt al-hisāb* (Problems of arithmetic). No copies of this work are in existence, but we know its content from two other sources—Khayyám's references to it in a later work and the detailed explanations given by Arabic mathematician Nasīr al-Dīn al-Tūsī in his book *Jāmi' al-hisāb bi'l-takht wa'l-turāb* (Collection on arithmetic by means of board and dust). Khayyám's arithmetic book introduced a new method for approximating roots of positive integers that improved on the methods the Hindus had developed. He proved the validity of his technique using algebraic proofs based on Euclid's *Elements*. As explained by al-Tūsī, to approximate the nth root of a positive integer N, Khayyám identified the largest possible integer a, for which $N \geq a^n$, and obtained his approximation from the computation

$$\sqrt[n]{N} \approx a + \frac{N - a^n}{(a+1)^n - a^n}$$. In order to calculate the value in the denomi-

nator of this expression efficiently, Khayyám used the binomial formula for the expansion of

$$\left(a+1\right)^n = a^n + na^{n-1} + \binom{n}{2}a^{n-2} + \binom{n}{3}a^{n-3} + \ldots + 1$$, a table of bino-

mial coefficients, and the recurring property that forms the basis of

Pascal's triangle, $\binom{n}{k} = \binom{n-1}{k} + \binom{n-1}{k-1}$. He had to explain these

ideas in words because the exponential notation of algebra and the symbols for the binomial coefficients had not yet been invented.

Khayyám's second mathematics book was an untitled treatise on algebra that has survived and has been translated into Persian, Russian, and English. In it he presented a classification of polynomial equations that could have positive roots. He identified 14 types of cubic equations—equations in which the highest-powered term was degree 3—based on the existence and arrangement of the positive coefficients in the lower-degree terms of the equation. In addition to the one equation having two terms, $x^3 = c$, he listed six equations having three terms

$x^3 + ax^2 = c$, $x^3 + c = ax^2$, $x^3 = ax^2 + c$, $x^3 + bx = c$, $x^3 + c = bx$, $x^3 = bx + c$

and seven equations having four terms

$x^3 + ax^2 = bx + c$, $x^3 + bx + c = ax^2$, $x^3 + bx = ax^2 + c$, $x^3 + ax^2 + c = bx$, $x^3 + c = ax^2 + bx$, $x^3 + ax^2 + bx = c$, $x^3 = ax^2 + bx + c$.

He noted that earlier mathematicians had given ruler-and-compass methods for solving four of these types of equations and that he was working to develop geometrical solutions for the other 10 variations.

The most advanced material in Khayyám's untitled algebra book was his solution to a particular cubic equation. He detailed a geometrical method for finding the one positive root of the equation $x^3 + 200x = 20x^2 + 2,000$, demonstrating that this root coincided with the point of intersection of the circle $(x - 15)^2 + y^2 = 25$ and the hyperbola $y = \dfrac{\sqrt{200}(x - 10)}{x}$. His numerical approximation for the root was within 1% of the actual value of $x \approx 15.43689$. Khayyám

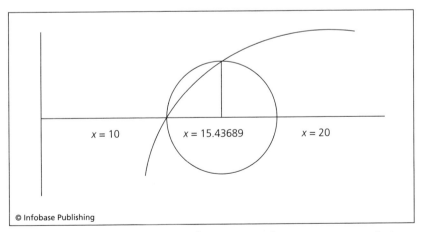

© Infobase Publishing

Khayyám solved the cubic equaton $x^3 + 200x = 20x^2 + 2,000$ geometrically by finding the intersection of the circle $(x - 15)^2 + y^2 = 25$ and the hyperbola $\dfrac{\sqrt{200}(x-10)}{x}$.

commented that, since the solution technique required the use of conic sections, the equation could not be solved by a more elementary ruler-and-compass construction. This insightful observation is the earliest-known assertion about the solvability of cubic equations. European mathematicians came to the same conclusion independently in the 17th century but did not prove the claim until the early 19th century.

Khayyám also wrote a book on the theory of music titled *al-Qāwl alā ajinās allatī bi'l-arba'a* (Discussion on genera contained in a fourth). This work addressed the problem of dividing a musical fourth into three intervals of tonalities—diatonic, chromatic, and enharmonic—a classic problem that Greek and Arabic scholars had discussed at length for 13 centuries. They had identified 19 intervals having the same ratio as the fourth. Khayyám discovered three additional ratios and evaluated the aesthetics of all 22 tones. Consistent with his other two books, his presentation included original contributions to a classic problem and demonstrated a thorough familiarity with the work of other scholars from his own country and from other cultures.

Geometrical Solutions of Cubic Equations

Around 1070, the chief justice Abu Tahir invited Khayyám to become a resident scholar at his court in Samarkand. Under this generous patronage, he wrote a third mathematics book titled *Risāla fī'l-barāhin 'alā masā'il al-jabr wa'l-muqābala* (Treatise on demonstration of problems by completion and balancing). The last part of the title refers to the two primary operations of algebra that al-Khwārizmī introduced in his seminal ninth-century text *al-Kitāb al-mukhtasar fī hisāb al-jabr wa'l-muqābala* (The compendious book on calculation by completion and balancing). In the introduction to his book, Khayyám gave one of the earliest definitions of algebra, specifying its purpose as determining integer and fractional solutions to relationships between quantities that are given as integers or as measurements. He explained that algebra was primarily focused on solving problems that arose from physical situations involving distances, areas, volumes, weights, and time. Since he did not envision its usefulness beyond applications in the three-dimensional world, the book addressed only linear, quadratic, and cubic equations.

In his *Risāla*, as the book has come to be known, Khayyám completed the work on geometrical solutions to cubic equations that he had started in his earlier untitled work. For each of the 14 types of cubic equations that he identified, he showed how to construct a circle and either a hyperbola or a parabola whose intersection provided one of the solutions of the cubic equation. He discussed situations in which an equation had no roots, one root, a double root, or two roots, but he failed to recognize the possibilities of a cubic equation having three distinct roots, such as $(x - 1)(x - 2)(x - 3) = 0$, or having a triple root, such as $(x - 1)^3 = 0$. He restricted his analysis exclusively to the consideration of positive coefficients and positive roots because mathematicians had not yet embraced the concept of negative numbers. Despite these deficiencies, mathematicians regarded his *Risāla* highly because it systematically provided geometrical solutions to all cubic equations, gave the earliest demonstration that a cubic equation could have more than one root, and reiterated his earlier assertion that cubic equations could not be solved by ruler-and-compass constructions.

Calendar Reform

In 1073, Toghrul Beg's grandson Jalāl al-Dīn Malik-shāh became sultan and established Isfahan as the capital of his empire. Khayyám accepted the new sultan's invitation to establish an observatory in Isfahan and spent 18 productive years there. He assembled a group of leading astronomers and organized them to compile the *Zīj Malik-shāhi* (Astronomical tables of Malik-shāh). This work included a catalog of the 100 brightest stars in the sky and tables of ecliptic coordinates indicating where the Sun would rise and set at different times of the year.

As requested by Malik-shāh, Khayyám directed a group of eight astronomers in an attempt to create a new calendar that would be more accurate than the Persian and Muslim calendars that were in use at the time. In 1079, after working on this project for five years, he produced a calendar called *al-ta'rīkh al-Jalālī*, meaning "Jalālī era," in honor of the sultan. He based the calendar on a cycle of 33 years that included eight leap years of 366 days and 25 regular years each having 365 days. With an average of 365.2424 days per year, this calendar was accurate to within one day every 5,000 years. Khayyám's calendar system not only represented a significant improvement over the calendars then in use; it was more accurate than the current Gregorian calendar introduced in 1582, which has an error of one day in 3,330 years.

Parallel Lines and Ratios

While working on his astronomy projects at the observatory, Khayyám continued to develop new mathematical ideas. In 1077, he published his fourth mathematical work, titled *Sharh ma ashkala min musādarāt kitāb Uqlīdes* (Commentaries on difficult postulates of Euclid's book). In book I of this three-volume work, Khayyám proposed a set of eight propositions to replace Euclid's parallel postulate. He proved that, given two lines that are both perpendicular to the same line, if they intersect on one side of that line, then, by symmetry, they must also intersect on the other side. From this result, he reasoned that the two perpendiculars cannot meet but cannot diverge either; they must remain equidistant from each other. Connecting the endpoints of two equal line segments on the perpendicular lines, he created a four-sided figure

© Infobase Publishing

The diagram Khayyám used to "prove" Euclid's parallel postulate predated the Saccheri quadrilateral by 600 years.

that he used to prove his remaining propositions, including his eighth proposition, in which he proved Euclid's parallel postulate. Although his logical reasoning was flawless, Khayyám had made an assumption at the beginning of his argument that was logically equivalent to the parallel postulate. Despite this defect, the conclusions that he deduced in his first two propositions formed the basis for the non-Euclidean geometries discovered in the 19th century by German Bernhard Riemann and Russian Nikolai Lobachevsky. Mathematicians refer to Khayyám's four-sided figure as the Saccheri quadrilateral, after Italian mathematician Giovanni Saccheri, who reintroduced this figure and a similar line of reasoning in the early 18th century.

In books II and III of his commentary on Euclid, Khayyám presented a detailed discussion of the theory of ratios and proportions. Euclid had presented a theory of ratios that was incomplete for incommensurable quantities. In the ninth century, Arabic mathematician al-Mahini had developed a competing theory of ratios based on continued fractions. Khayyám proved that the two theories of ratios were equivalent and showed how that equivalence enabled one to multiply ratios. Like his theory of parallel lines, Khayyám's work on ratios influenced the work of later Arabic mathematicians but had little impact on the development of European mathematics because his works were not discovered and translated until the 19th century.

Philosophical Writings

During his years at the observatory, Khayyám produced three works on philosophy at the request of high-ranking governmental officials. In 1080, he wrote *Risāla al-kawn wa'l-taklīf* (Treatise on being and duty), in which he discussed the creation of the world and humanity's responsibility to pray. His second work, titled *Al-Jawab 'an thalāth masā'il: darūrat al-tadadd fī'l-'ālam wa'l-jabr wa'l-baqā* (Answer to three questions: On the necessity of contradiction in the world, on determinism, and on longevity), presented various perspectives about the three issues cited in its title. His third philosophical work of the period, titled *Risāla fī'l kulliyat al-wujūd* (Treatise on the universality of existence), addressed existential questions of being. In each philosophical work, Khayyám tailored the content to coincide with the religious and philosophical beliefs of the patron who sponsored the project. He drew from the writings of other philosophers but only rarely endorsed or debated their positions. He authored two additional philosophical works, titled *Risāla al-diyā' al-'aqlī fī mawdū' al 'ilm al-kullī* (The light of reason on the subject of universal science) and *Risāla fi'l wujūd* (Treatise on existence), that cannot be accurately dated.

When sultan Malik-shāh died in 1092, his successors withdrew all financial support for the observatory and for general scientific research. Although Khayyám remained at the Seljuk court, he fell out of favor with the new rulers. In an attempt to convince them to renew their support for mathematics, science, and astronomy, he wrote a work titled *Naurūz-nāma*, in which he described the ancient Iranian festival of Naurūz that celebrated the solar new year. In this book, he also presented a history of the calendar reforms that had been sponsored by previous rulers whom he portrayed favorably. His efforts failed to persuade the rulers.

Around 1120, Khayyám moved to Merv, the new Seljuk capital, where he wrote two works that blended philosophy and physics. In *Mizān al-hikam* (Balance of wisdoms), he gave an algebraic solution to the problem of determining the composition of an alloy of gold and silver. Familiar with Archimedes' solution to a similar problem about a king's crown, he described a process of submerging the alloy into water, measuring the amount of water displaced, and using the specific gravity of each metal to determine the proportional composition of the alloy. In *Fī'l-qustas al-mustaqīm* (On right qustas), he discussed weighing objects using a special type of scale having movable weights. His analysis of this physical situation again built on Archimedes' theory of balance and levers.

Rubáiyát (Quatrains)

Khayyám's most widely known writings are his poems. The lack of an authoritative collection of his poetry makes it difficult to determine when he wrote his poems and which poems attributed to him were actually his work. He wrote an extensive collection of four-line poems, or quatrains, each of which was called a *ruba'i*—a poetic

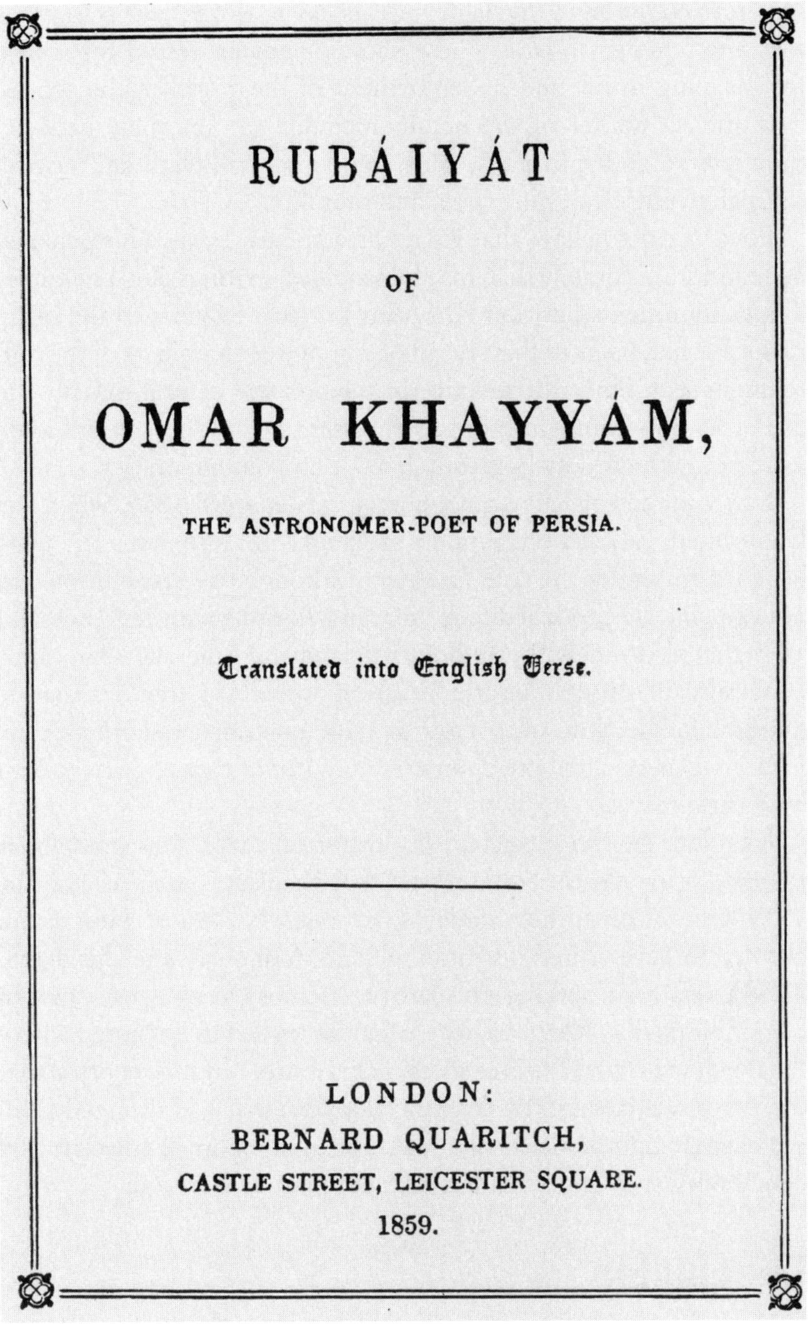

RUBÁIYÁT

OF

OMAR KHAYYÁM,

THE ASTRONOMER-POET OF PERSIA.

Translated into English Verse.

LONDON:

BERNARD QUARITCH,

CASTLE STREET, LEICESTER SQUARE.

1859.

Edward Fitzgerald's collection of Khayyám's poetry titled the *Rubáiyát* (Quatrains) circulated widely in Western cultures during the late 19th century. *(The Granger Collection)* structure common in Persia during his day in which each stanza has a rhyme scheme of *aaba*. These short poems expressed his search for meaning in life and his enjoyment of the world of the senses. The subject matter of the poems included the interplay between the material and spiritual worlds, good and evil, truth and justice, sensual pleasures, destiny, fate, and morality.

Poetry critics believe that Khayyám's poems revealed his personal beliefs more accurately than his philosophical writings did. Their irreligious sentiments position Khayyám in sharp contrast to the other major Persian poets of this era, all of whom were members of the Súfi religious sect. Since the practice of religion was central to daily life in Persia at the time, his poems expressing his countercultural ideas were not embraced by large numbers of his contemporaries.

Few volumes of Khayyám's poetry existed until 1859, when the Englishman Edward Fitzgerald translated 75 of his poems and published them under the title *Rubáiyát*. Although the first edition was not popular, he produced four enlarged editions between 1868 and 1889 that sold widely throughout England and America. Khayyám's fame spread throughout the Western world as other translators published collections of as many as 1,100 quatrains under his name. Literary experts attribute approximately 120 of these poems to him with certainty.

Khayyám died in Nīshābūr, but historical sources disagree about the date of his death. Some report that he died as early as 1123 or 1124. One of his former students, Khwájah Nizámi of Samarkand, claimed to have visited his tomb in 1135, four years after his death. Another historian specifies the date precisely as December 4, 1131. In one of his poems, Khayyám wrote that he wished to be buried where the north wind could scatter roses on his grave. Nizámi reported that the grave was covered by fragrant blossoms that had dropped from the overhanging branches of a fruit tree growing in an adjacent garden. Today an elegant shrine marks the place of his tomb.

Conclusion

Omar Khayyám distinguished himself as one of the leading Persian scholars of his day, excelling in the fields of mathematics, astronomy, philosophy, the physical sciences, and poetry. His most significant mathematical work provided systematic geometrical solutions to cubic equations. His commentaries on Euclid's theories of parallel lines and ratios were important achievements in geometry and arithmetic. Each of these new developments advanced the work started by the ancient Greeks and was further developed by generations of Arabic mathematicians. Khayyám's writings were largely unavailable outside the Arabic world until the 19th century, by which time European mathematicians had independently rediscovered and further extended most of his ideas. When his works were examined by Western scholars, they provided insight into the advanced state of mathematics attained by Arabic scholars of his era.

FURTHER READING

Coolidge, Julian L. "Omar Khayyám." In *The Mathematics of Great Amateurs*, 19–29. London: Oxford University Press, 1949. Biographical sketch and discussion of Khayyám's mathematical works.

Fitzgerald, Edward. *Rubáiyát of Omar Khayyám*. Garden City, N.Y.: Garden City Publishing, 1937. Brief biographical sketch followed by English translation of Khayyám's poetry.

Katz, Victor J. "Chapter 7. The Mathematics of Islam." In *A History of Mathematics: An Introduction*. 2nd ed. 238–287. Reading, Mass.: Addison Wesley Longmann, 1998. Chapter from college textbook explains some of Khayyám's mathematical works and provides brief biographical sketch.

Minderovic, Zoran. "Omar Khayyam." In *Notable Mathematicians from Ancient Times to the Present*, edited by Robin V. Young, 272–273. Detroit: Gale, 1998. Brief biography.

O'Connor, J. J., and E. F. Robertson. "Omar Khayyam." In "MacTutor History of Mathematics Archive." University of Saint Andrews. Available online. URL: http://turnbull.mcs.st-and.ac.uk/~history/Mathematicians/Khayyam.html. Accessed March 25, 2005. Online biography, from the University of Saint Andrews, Scotland.

Reimer, Luetta, and Wilbert Reimer. "A Fortune Shared: Omar Khayyam." In *Mathematicians Are People, Too: Stories from the Lives of Great Mathematicians*. Vol. 2, 8–15. Parsippany, N.J.:

Seymour, 1995. Life story with historical facts and fictionalized dialogue; intended for elementary school students.

Youschkevitvch, A. P., and B. A. Rosenfeld. "al-Khayyāmī (or Khayyām), Ghiyāth al-Dīn Abū'l-Fath 'Umar ibn Ibrāhīm al-Nīshābūri." In *Dictionary of Scientific Biography*. Vol. 7, edited by Charles C. Gillispie, 323–334. New York: Scribner, 1972. Detailed encyclopedic biography.

Leonardo Fibonacci

(ca. 1175–ca. 1250 C.E.)

Leonardo Fibonacci helped to introduce the Hindu-Arabic number system in Europe and to revive an interest in classical Greek mathematics. *(The Granger Collection)*

Hindu-Arabic Numerals in Europe

The most talented and influential mathematician during Europe's Middle Ages was Leonardo Fibonacci (pronounced fib-o-NAT-chee). A master of computational techniques, his writings played a significant role in introducing the Hindu-Arabic number system to European culture. His books helped to rediscover the classical mathematics of the Greeks and Arabs and to advance the branch of mathematics known as number theory. He is best remembered for a sequence of numbers that he used to solve a riddle about rabbits.

Early Years

Fibonacci was born in Pisa, Italy, around the year 1175. The name Fibonacci means "son of Bonacci" or "member of the Bonacci family." At times, he was called Leonardo of Pisa, Leonardo Pisano, or Leonardo Pisani, after the place of his birth. Later in his career, he also referred to himself as Leonardo Bigollo or Leonardo Bigoli, meaning "the traveler" or "the blockhead."

Guilielmo Bonacci, Fibonacci's father, served as secretary of the Republic of Pisa, an independent city-state with a population of 10,000 located on the banks of the Arno River in the region of central Italy known as Tuscany. In 1192, he became director of the customhouse in Bugia, a Pisan trading colony on the coast of northern Africa. As a teenager, Fibonacci joined his father in Bugia and traveled with him for 10 years to commercial cities in Greece, Turkey, Syria, Egypt, France, and Sicily. As he trained to become a merchant, Fibonacci learned to negotiate contracts, to determine fair prices for goods, and to convert money from the currency of one country to that of another.

Fibonacci obtained an extensive education from Muslim instructors in Bugia and from scholars in the Mediterranean cities to which he traveled. In addition to the classical Greek mathematics discovered by Pythagoras, Euclid, and Archimedes, they taught him the advancements made by Indian scholars like Āryabhata and Brahmagupta and the more recent work of Arabic writers like Omar Khayyám and Muhammad al-Khwārizmī. The Indian and Arabic mathematical discoveries that he learned were largely unknown in Europe, where cultural and technological advancement had stagnated for 700 years during the Dark Ages.

Hindu-Arabic Numbering System

Fibonacci recognized that Arabic merchants were utilizing mathematical techniques that were superior to those commonly used in most European countries. They had a more efficient system for representing whole numbers and fractions. With this system they could work with numbers of any magnitude, perform written computations, and check the accuracy of their work systematically.

Most Europeans used Roman numerals, a numbering system introduced around 500 B.C.E. during the early Roman Empire, in which the seven letters I, V, X, L, C, D, and M corresponded to the values 1, 5, 10, 50, 100, 500, and 1000. A combination of symbols represented the sum of the values of the individual letters; CCLXVIII represented 100 + 100 + 50 + 10 + 5 + 1 + 1 + 1 = 268. Certain letter pairs indicated subtraction, with an X to the left of a C indicating "10 less than 100" and an I before a V standing for "one less than five." In this manner, DXCIV represented the value 500 + (100 − 10) + (5 − 1) = 594. Placing a bar above a symbol or enclosing a symbol in parentheses increased its value by a factor of 1,000; $\overline{V}$ represented 5,000 and (C) represented 100,000.

Arabic countries used a numbering system that the Hindus in India had developed and refined between 300 B.C.E. and 700 C.E. This system used 10 symbols and a place-value notation to represent quantities as sums of powers of 10. A symbol like our zero indicated that there were no groups of a certain size. This feature allowed the same symbol, such as "4," to represent four, 40, 400, or 4,000, depending on its position within the digits of the number. In this manner, 4,304 represented $(4 \times 1000) + (3 \times 100) + (0 \times 0) + (4 \times 1)$. The Arabic countries adopted this system, revised some of the symbols, and produced the familiar numbers of the current Hindu-Arabic numbering system—0, 1, 2, 3, 4, 5, 6, 7, 8, 9.

Fibonacci realized that arithmetic was much easier with this numbering system. He learned how to add, subtract, multiply, and divide efficiently using the Hindu-Arabic numbers and how to write the computations on paper. With Roman numerals, addition and subtraction were cumbersome, multiplication and division were very difficult, and there was no method for writing down the steps in a computation. Most Europeans recorded their final answer in Roman numerals but did their calculations with an abacus—an ancient calculating tool invented hundreds of years earlier in China consisting of a collection of beads on pieces of wire organized into columns within a frame.

A woodcut titled *Typus arithmeticae* (Methods of arithmetic) dating from 1503 depicts Boethius calculating with Hindu-Arabic numerals and Pythagoras working with a counting board similar to an abacus. *(Library of Congress, Prints and Photographs Division)*

Liber Abaci (Book of Computation)

Fibonacci returned to Pisa, where in 1202 he wrote *Liber abaci* (Book of computation), a work designed to promote the advantages of the Hindu-Arabic numbering system. In this handwritten Latin manuscript, the first seven chapters explained how to perform arithmetic calculations with the new numbering system. The next four chapters showed how these techniques made it easy to perform many common business transactions. The final four chapters presented techniques from arithmetic, algebra, geometry, and number theory and their use in solving a variety of problems and mathematical puzzles.

In his organized presentation of the mechanics of the Hindu-Arabic numbering system, Fibonacci stressed straightforward methods, error checking, and efficiency. After explaining how to read and write numbers with the digits organized into groups of three, he showed how to multiply, add, subtract, and divide whole numbers, fractions, and mixed numbers. He explained how to use "hand figures" to remember the carry digits temporarily when multiplying or adding. With all whole-number calculations, he showed how to check the results by "casting out nines"—a procedure in which one compared the sum of the digits of the final result with the sums of the digits of the numbers being combined. For fractions and mixed numbers, he presented notations in which the fraction $\dfrac{1\ 5\ 7}{2\ 6\ 10}$ represented the sum of the fractions

$\dfrac{1}{2 \cdot 6 \cdot 10} + \dfrac{5}{6 \cdot 10} + \dfrac{7}{10}$ and the mixed number $\dfrac{3\ 12}{7\ 13}\ 9$ represented

the sum $\dfrac{3}{7 \cdot 13} + \dfrac{12}{13} + 9$. He concluded the section on arithmetic by

showing how to write a fraction as a sum of unit fractions—frac-

tions having numerators of one—such as $\dfrac{20}{33} = \dfrac{1}{66} + \dfrac{1}{11} + \dfrac{1}{2}$.

The middle chapters of *Liber abaci* explained how this new numbering system made it easier to do common business transactions, including computing interest, calculating profits, discounting prices, converting currency, administering partnerships, and alloying money. For each type of problem, Fibonacci showed how to perform the computations on paper using the relevant arithmetic techniques from the previous chapters. In the style of an experienced teacher, he explained each concept using clear examples with complete and detailed solutions.

The final four chapters applied the new computational techniques to the solutions of mathematical puzzles and more advanced applications. Chapter 12, comprising a third of the entire book, presented a variety of entertaining puzzles and riddles that Fibonacci had borrowed from the earlier writings of Greek, Arabic, Egyptian, Chinese, and Indian mathematicians. These mathematical amusements ranged from spiders climbing walls, dogs chasing rabbits, and people buying horses to determining the number of grains of rice on a chessboard or the amount of money in a coin purse. He explained the methods of false position and double false position and showed how they could be used to solve all the types of problems presented earlier in the book. In the final chapter, he explained algebraic and geometrical techniques that al-Khwārizmī and Euclid had developed.

Liber abaci was one of the most influential mathematical works written during the Middle Ages. Fibonacci's thorough explanations of the mechanics of computation using the Hindu-Arabic number system and his demonstration of the many applied problems that could be solved easily using these techniques were persuasive. His book and similar works by Frenchman Alexandre de Villedieu and Englishman John of Halifax, also known as Sacrobosco, convinced businessmen, scientists, government officials, and teachers throughout Europe to discontinue the use of Roman numerals and to adopt the superior Hindu-Arabic number system for almost all calculating and record-keeping purposes. The work also established Fibonacci's reputation as a leading scholar among his contemporaries.

In addition to presenting useful computational techniques and practical mathematical applications, Fibonacci introduced in *Liber abaci* two original ideas—single-letter variables and negative numbers. Throughout most of the book, he followed the Greek tradition of expressing each equation in words referring to the unknown quantity as *res*, meaning "thing." Beginning in chapter nine, he used single letters for unspecified numbers in the explanations of computations and for some lengths in geometrical problems. These are the earliest-known instances of the use of single-letter variables to represent general quantities. In the solutions of "men and purse" problems, he used negative numbers that resulted from subtracting a larger quantity from a smaller one and showed that adding such a "debit" was equivalent to subtracting the corresponding positive number. Although most European countries embraced the Hindu-Arabic numbering system by the late 13th century, mathematicians did not widely adopt either of these practices until the late 16th century.

Fibonacci Series

Fibonacci's name is associated with an infinite sequence of numbers that he used to solve one of the puzzles presented in *Liber abaci*. The numbers 1, 2, 3, 5, 8, 13, 21, 34, 55, 89, etc., follow a well-defined pattern: after the first two numbers in the sequence, each subsequent number is the sum of the two numbers that precede it. For example, the number occurring after 5 and 8 is 5 + 8 = 13; the number after 34 and 55 is 34 + 55 = 89. Mathematicians describe this pattern using the recurrence relation $F_n = F_{n-1} + F_{n-2}$, which indicates that the nth number is the sum of the two previous numbers.

Fibonacci presented the series as the solution to a puzzle titled "How Many Pairs of Rabbits Are Created by One Pair in One Year." The puzzle asked the solver to determine how many pairs of rabbits a farmer would have after 12 months under the following circumstances:

> A pair of adult rabbits produces a pair of offspring at the end of each month. Each new pair reproduces beginning at the end of their second month. If a farmer starts with a single pair of adult rabbits, how many pairs will he have at the end of a year?

The terms of the series give the number of pairs of rabbits that the farmer has at the end of each month. The initial pair of rabbits ($F_0 = 1$) produces a second pair by the end of the first month ($F_1 = 2$). In the second month, the baby rabbits mature, and the original pair reproduces again ($F_2 = 3$). At the end of the third month, the two pairs of mature rabbits reproduce, increasing the total number of rabbits to five pairs ($F_3 = 5$). In general, the number of pairs of newborn rabbits that are added to the collection at the end of each month is the same as the number of pairs of rabbits that are at least two months old ($F_n = F_{n-1} + F_{n-2}$). Following this pattern, Fibonacci showed that at the end of the 12th month, the farmer will have $F_{12} = F_{11} + F_{10} = 233 + 144 = 377$ pairs of rabbits.

Mathematicians who studied this series of numbers in later years added an additional "1" to the beginning of the series and renumbered the terms to start with F_1. These modifications allowed them to calculate the nth term of the resulting "Fibonacci series" 1, 1, 2, 3, 5, 8, 13, 21, etc., using the formula $F_n = \dfrac{1}{\sqrt{5}}\left[\left(\dfrac{1+\sqrt{5}}{2}\right)^n - \left(\dfrac{1-\sqrt{5}}{2}\right)^n\right]$.

Mathematical Tournament

In 1220, Fibonacci published a second book titled *Practica geometriae* (Practical geometry). In this work, he solved problems involving lengths, area, and volumes of two- and three-dimensional geometrical figures. Emphasizing practical applications, he explained techniques by which surveyors could determine the area of a field lying on the side of a hill or the height of a tall tree. He also presented techniques for calculating square and cube roots to any desired degree of accuracy and methods for determining the dimensions of polygons, such as a square inscribed in a triangle. As he did with his first book, he borrowed much of his material from books that had been written by Greek and Arabic mathematicians. Nine copies of this book still exist today.

Emperor Frederick II, who was the king of Germany and the Holy Roman Emperor, learned of Fibonacci's reputation as a mathematical scholar. He requested that Fibonacci participate in a mathematical tournament during the emperor's visit to Pisa. Johannes of Palermo, a member of the emperor's staff, created a set of three challenging problems and invited several well-known mathematicians to take part in the competition. Fibonacci solved all three problems correctly while none of the other competitors solved any.

In 1225, Fibonacci presented his solutions to the three tournament problems in a short book titled *Incipit flos Leonardo bigoli pisani super solutionibus quarumdam questionum ad numerum et ad geometriam vel ad utrumque pertinentium* (Here begins the flower of Leonardo Bigoli of Pisa on the solutions to certain questions pertaining to number and geometry or to either of them). The first tournament problem asked the solver to find three fractions whose squares were spaced five units apart. Stated in modern algebraic notation, one needed to find fractions x, y, and z, satisfying the equations $x^2 = y^2 - 5$ and $z^2 = y^2 + 5$. Without explaining how he obtained the answer, Fibonacci demonstrated that the solutions were $x = \frac{31}{12}, y = \frac{41}{12},$ and $y = \frac{49}{12}$. The second tournament problem asked to find a number x for which $x^3 + 2x^2 + 10x = 20$. Fibonacci knew that the Greek mathematician Euclid had proven that no integer or fraction satisfied this equation. Although he could not find the exact answer, Fibonacci gave an approximate solution $x = 1 + \frac{22}{60} + \frac{7}{60^2} + \frac{42}{60^3} + \frac{33}{60^4} + \frac{4}{60^5} + \frac{40}{60^6}$. This number is so close to the actual answer that when it is written in decimal form as 1.3688081075 . . . , the first nine digits after the decimal point match the digits of the correct answer. The third tournament problem was a puzzle involving three men who owned a half, a third, and a sixth of a sum of money. Fibonacci provided a simple solution for this seemingly complicated problem using techniques that he had presented in *Liber abaci* for similar "men and purse" problems.

Liber Quadratorum (Book of the Square)

Later that same year, Fibonacci published another book, titled *Liber quadratorum* (Book of the square), that he dedicated to the emperor. In this work on number theory, he explained how to solve equations involving quantities raised to the second power. He showed several techniques for generating infinitely many Pythagorean triples, sets of integers x, y, and z for which $x^2 + y^2 = z^2$. One of these techniques used the identity $(a^2 + b^2)(c^2 + d^2) = (ac + bd)^2 + (ad - bc)^2 = (ac - bd)^2 + (ad + bc)^2$. Although Greek and Arab mathematicians had written about this identity hundreds of years earlier, it became known as Fibonacci's identity.

In another section of the book, Fibonacci introduced a class of numbers he called congruums, which are integers of the form $n = ab(a + b)(a - b)$ if $a + b$ is even and $n = 4ab(a + b)(a - b)$ if $a + b$ is odd. With a series of logical proofs, he developed many properties of these numbers, including the proofs that every congruum is divisible by 24 and that the square root of a congruum cannot be an integer. He proved that if $y^2 + n$ and $y^2 - n$ were perfect squares, then n had to be a congruum. With $y = 41$ and $n = 720$, he showed how this result could be used to solve the first tournament problem.

Although during his lifetime Fibonacci was better known for his *Liber abaci*, later mathematicians regarded *Liber quadratorum* as a more significant accomplishment. The earlier book demonstrated that he was a persuasive writer and had mastered the classical mathematics of the Greeks, Arabs, and Hindus. The later work showed that in the next 20 years he had become a mathematician who had advanced to topics far beyond arithmetic computation. In this work, he organized the major results in number theory that had been obtained by earlier mathematicians and extended this knowledge using additional techniques and concepts. The new mathematical theories and methods of solution that he introduced made his *Liber quadratorum* the leading book on number theory for the next 400 years.

Other Works

Fibonacci produced two other mathematical works that no longer exist. *Di minor guisa* (In a lesser way) was a book on commercial arithmetic, probably similar to the middle chapters from *Liber abaci*, in which he explained how to perform common business transactions with the Hindu-Arabic numbering system. He also wrote a commentary on Book X of Euclid's *Elements*, in which he presented a numerical treatment of irrational numbers extending Euclid's geometrical presentation. Other contemporary writers mentioned this work, but no copies of it exist, and the exact title is not known.

In 1228, Fibonacci published a revised second edition of *Liber abaci*, in which he added some new material and removed some that he thought was less important. Twelve copies of this manuscript dating from the 13th to the 15th centuries still exist. Since no copies of the 1202 edition survived, it is not possible to determine how the editions differ. Fibonacci dedicated the 1228 edition to Michael Scot, an author of several science textbooks and the emperor's chief astrologist.

During the last years of Fibonacci's life, he served the government of Pisa, advising them on matters of finance and accounting. In 1240, the Republic of Pisa honored him as a distinguished citizen and provided him an annual bonus in addition to his regular salary. He died around the year 1250.

Conclusion

Fibonacci was the most influential mathematician of the Middle Ages. Through his book *Liber abaci*, he helped to convince Europeans to adopt the Hindu-Arabic number system. His use of negative numbers and single-letter variables anticipated major advances in algebra by several centuries. For four centuries after his death, his book *Liber quadratorum* presented the most advanced treatment of number theory. His entire body of work helped Europeans to rediscover the classical mathematics of the Greeks and Arabs. Throughout the last eight centuries, his collection of number puzzles has intrigued authors of books on recreational mathematics as well as serious mathematicians.

The Fibonacci series 1, 1, 2, 3, 5, 8, 13, 21, 34 . . . that evolved from the rabbit problem has become the subject of intense study by mathematicians and scientists. They have determined that the ratios of successive terms in the series approach the golden mean $\phi = \frac{\sqrt{5}+1}{2} \approx 1.618$, a special constant that had interested the ancient Greeks. Biologists have observed pairs of consecutive Fibonacci numbers in the opposing spirals of the scales on pineapples and pine cones and of the seeds in sunflowers and daisies as well as in the arrangement of leaves on flower stems. In 1963, mathematicians who investigate properties of Fibonacci numbers, Lucas numbers, and other recursive number sequences formed the Fibonacci Association and created a journal called *The Fibonacci Quarterly*, in which they publish their research results.

FURTHER READING

Biswas, Asit K., and Margaret R. Peitsch. "Fibonacci, Leonardo, or Leonardo of Pisa." In *Dictionary of Scientific Biography*. Vol. 4, edited by Charles C. Gillispie, 604–614. New York: Scribner, 1972. Detailed encyclopedic biography.

O'Connor, J. J., and E. F. Robertson. "Leonardo Pisano Fibonacci." In "MacTutor History of Mathematics Archive." University of Saint Andrews. Available online. URL: http://turnbull.mcs. st-and.ac.uk/~history/Mathematicians/Fibonacci.html. Accessed March 25, 2005. Online biography, from the University of Saint Andrews, Scotland.

Reimer, Luetta, and Wilbert Reimer. "Lean on the Blockhead: Leonard of Pisa (Fibonacci)." In *Mathematicians Are People, Too: Stories from the Lives of Great Mathematicians*. Vol. 2, 16–23. Parsippany, N.J.: Seymour, 1995. Life story with historical facts and fictionalized dialogue; intended for elementary school students.

Reinherz, Leslie. "Leonardo Pisano Fibonacci." In *Notable Mathematicians from Ancient Times to the Present*, edited by Robin V. Young, 177–179. Detroit: Gale, 1998. Brief biography.

Sigler, L. E. *Fibonacci's "Liber Abaci": Leonardo Pisano's "Book of Calculation."* New York: Springer, 2002. English translation of Fibonacci's influential mathematical work.

GLOSSARY

abundant number An integer such as 12 that is less than the sum of its factors. Also known as an OVER-PERFECT NUMBER.

acoustici The lower level of students in the Pythagorean Society known as the listeners who attended lectures but could not ask questions; they learned solely by listening, observing, and thinking.

acoustics The study of sound.

algebra The branch of mathematics dealing with the manipulation of variables and equations.

algebraic expression An expression built up out of numbers and variables using the operations of addition, subtraction, multiplication, division, raising to a power, and taking a root.

amicable numbers See FRIENDLY NUMBERS.

angle A planar figure formed by two rays with a common endpoint.

arc The portion of the circumference of a circle between two specified points.

Archimedean principle of buoyancy The law of hydrostatics discovered by Archimedes of Syracuse that states: when an object is placed into a liquid, the weight of the object will be reduced by the weight of the liquid that it replaces.

Archimedean screw See WATER SCREW.

Archimedean spiral A spiral traced out by a point rotating about a fixed point at a constant angular speed while simultaneously moving away from the fixed point at a constant speed. It is given in polar coordinates by $r = a\theta$, where a is a positive constant.

arithmetic The study of computation.

arithmetic series An infinite sum of the form $a + (a + r) + (a + 2r) + (a + 3r) + \ldots$

astrolabe A mechanical device used to measure the inclination of a star or other object of observation.

astrology A mystical theory that explains how a person's personality and fate are determined by the positions of the stars and planets at the time he or she was born.

astronomy The study of stars, planets, and other heavenly bodies.

axiom A statement giving a property of an undefined term or a relationship between undefined terms. The axioms of a specific mathematical theory govern the behavior of the undefined terms in that theory; they are assumed to be true and cannot be proved. Also known as a POSTULATE.

binomial coefficient A positive integer given by the computation $\binom{n}{k} = \dfrac{n!}{k!(n-k)!}$, where n and k are integers satisfying $0 \leq k \leq n$.

bisect To divide into two congruent pieces, as a line segment or a circle.

central angle An angle formed by two radii of the same circle.

chord A line segment whose two endpoints lie on a circle.

circle The set of all points in a plane at a given distance (the radius) from a fixed point (the center).

circumference (1) The points on a circle. (2) The measure of the total arc length of a circle; it is 2π times the radius of the circle.

circumscribed polygon A polygon, with each edge tangent to the circumference of a circle.

commensurable Having a common measure. Two segments or numbers are commensurable if their ratio is a fraction of two whole numbers.

commentary An edited version of a book in which material has been revised, corrected, updated, or expanded.

composite number A positive integer that can be factored as the product of two or more primes.

cone The surface swept out by a line that is rotated about an axis while keeping one point (the vertex) fixed.

congruent polygons Two polygons for which there is a one-to-one correspondence between angles and sides, with corresponding angles congruent and corresponding sides equal in length.

conic Any one of the curved shapes—ellipse, parabola, and hyperbola—obtained by the intersection of a plane with a cone. Also known as a CONIC SECTION.

conic section See CONIC.

constellation A group of stars that appears to be arranged as the outline of the shape of an animal or a person.

cosine For an acute angle in a right triangle, the ratio of the adjacent side to the hypotenuse.

cube (1) A regular solid having six congruent faces, each of which is a square. (2) To multiply a quantity times itself three times; raise to the third power.

cyclic quadrilateral A four-sided plane figure whose vertices all lie on the circumference of a circle.

cylinder A solid with two congruent bases (usually circles) connected by a lateral surface generated by segments connecting corresponding points on the two bases.

decimal Base-10.

decimal fraction A fraction whose denominator is a power of 10.

deficient number An integer such as 15 that is greater than the sum of its factors.

degree (1) A unit of angle measure equal to 1/360 of a circle. (2) The number of edges that meet at a vertex in a polygon or polyhedron.

degree of a polynomial The highest exponent occurring in any of the terms of the polynomial.

diagonal In a square or a rectangle, the line joining two opposite corners.

diameter (1) The distance across a circle. (2) A line segment of this length passing through the center of a circle joining two points on opposite sides of the circle.

dodecahedron A regular solid having 12 congruent faces, each of which is a regular pentagon.

eclipse An astronomical event that occurs when the Sun, Earth, and Moon align and either the Moon disappears as it passes into the shadow cast by the Earth (lunar eclipse) or the Sun disappears as the Earth passes into the shadow cast by the Moon (solar eclipse).

Elements The influential book on geometry and number theory written by Euclid of Alexandria.

ellipse The intersection of a cone with a plane that meets the cone in a closed curve. Equivalently, the set of points whose distances from two fixed points, called the foci of the ellipse, have a constant sum.

epicyclic orbit An orbital path in which a celestial body revolves in a small circular path as it travels along a larger circular orbit about the Earth or another celestial body.

equator The circle on the surface of the Earth that is the intersection of the Earth with the plane that is perpendicular to the north-south axis and bisects that axis.

equinoxes The days in the spring (vernal equinox) and fall (autumnal equinox) when sunrise and sunset are 12 hours apart.

Euclidean algorithm The technique discovered by Euclid of Alexandria for determining the greatest common divisor of a pair of numbers.

Euclidean geometry The mathematical system of geometry derived from the five postulates assumed by Euclid of Alexandria.

even number An integer that can be written as two times another integer.

exhaustion, method of A method of computing the perimeter, area, or volume of a figure by approximating it with a sequence of inscribed polygons or polyhedra.

factor An integer that divides a given integer without leaving a remainder.

Fibonacci sequence A sequence of integers beginning 1, 1, 2, 3, 5, 8, 13, 21, etc., in which each number is the sum of the two numbers immediately preceding it.

fifth A pleasant-sounding musical chord produced by two strings that are 3/4 as long as each other.

fifth postulate See PARALLEL POSTULATE.

fourth A pleasant-sounding musical chord produced by two strings that are 2/3 as long as each other.

friendly numbers A pair of integers, such as 220 and 284, each one equal to the sum of the other's factors. Also known as AMI-CABLE NUMBERS.

geometric series An infinite sum of the form $a + ar + ar^2 + ar^3 + \ldots$

geometry The mathematical study of shapes, forms, their transformation, and the spaces that contain them.

gnomon A vertical pole used to create a triangle in order to determine a distance.

golden mean See GOLDEN SECTION.

golden ratio See GOLDEN SECTION.

golden section The cutting of a segment AB by a point P such that AB/AP = AP/BP. This ratio, known as the GOLDEN RATIO or GOLDEN MEAN, has a value of $\dfrac{1+\sqrt{5}}{2} \approx 1.618$.

greatest common divisor For two given integers, the largest number that divides both of them without leaving a remainder.

Harmony of the Spheres Pythagoras's theory that the motions of the seven heavenly bodies—the Moon, Mercury, Venus, the Sun, Mars, Jupiter, and Saturn—produced a natural musical harmony that coincided with the seven musical notes A through G.

hemisphere Half of a sphere.

hexagon A polygon with six sides.

Hindu-Arabic numbering system The base-10 place-value system of counting using the numerals 0, 1, 2, 3, 4, 5, 6, 7, 8, and 9 that was developed by Hindu mathematicians in India and Islamic mathematicians in the Arabic countries.

hydrometer An instrument used to measure the density (or specific gravity) of a liquid by comparing it to an equal volume of water.

hyperbola The intersection of a cone with a plane that intersects both nappes of the cone. Equivalently, the set of points whose distances from two fixed points, called the foci of the hyperbola, have a constant difference.

icosahedron A regular solid having 20 congruent faces, each of which is an equilateral triangle.

incommensurable See IRRATIONAL NUMBER.

inscribed polygon A polygon whose vertices are all on the circumference of a circle.

integer A whole number, such as –4, –1, 0, 2, or 5.

intersect To cross or meet.

irrational number A real number such as $\sqrt{2}$ or π that cannot be expressed as a ratio of two integers. Also known as an INCOMMENSURABLE.

isosceles triangle A triangle in which two sides are congruent.

latitude A circle on the surface of the Earth that is the intersection of the Earth with a plane perpendicular to the north-south axis.

longitude A semicircle on the surface of the Earth that is the intersection of the Earth with a half-plane whose edge is the north-south axis of the Earth.

mathematici The higher level of students in the Pythagorean Society known as the mathematicians who had obtained enough knowledge to ask questions and express their own opinions.

minute A unit of angle measure equal to 1/60th of a degree.

natural philosophy The branch of philosophy concerned with investigating the laws of nature that explain physical phenomena.

negative number Any number whose value is less than zero.

non-Euclidean geometry A mathematical system of geometry that results from substituting different assumptions in place of the parallel postulate.

number theory The mathematical study of the properties of positive integers.

numerology A mixture of arithmetic, mysticism, and magic.

oblong number A positive integer that can be written as $n(n + 1)$ for some integer n.

octahedron A regular solid having eight congruent faces, each of which is an equilateral triangle.

odd number An integer that is not an even integer. An integer that cannot be written as two times another integer.

orbit The path of one heavenly body around another, such as the Moon's orbit around the Earth or the Earth's orbit around the Sun.

over-perfect number See ABUNDANT NUMBER.

parabola The intersection of a cone with a plane that intersects one nappe of the cone but not in a closed curve. Equivalently, the set of points equidistant from a fixed point, called the focus of the parabola, and from a fixed line called the directrix of the parabola.

parallel lines Two lines in a plane are parallel if they do not intersect.

parallelogram A four-sided polygon in which both pairs of opposite sides are parallel.

parallel postulate The axiom stated by Euclid of Alexandria that for a given point and line, there is only one line that can be drawn through the point that does not eventually meet the other line. Also known as the FIFTH POSTULATE.

Pascal's triangle Rows of positive integers arranged in a triangular format in which the first and last entry in each row are 1, and each entry is the sum of the two entries above it.

pentagon A polygon with five sides.

pentagram The five-pointed star consisting of the five diagonals of a regular pentagon. It was the symbol of the Pythagorean Society.

perfect number A positive integer such as 6, 28, 496, and 8128 that is equal to the sum of its factors.

perfect square See SQUARE NUMBER.

perimeter The sum of the lengths of the sides of a polygon.

perpendicular Meeting at right angles.

philosophy The study of the meaning of life.

pi (π) The ratio of the circumference of a circle to its diameter, approximately 3.14159.

Platonic solids The five REGULAR SOLIDS—tetrahedron, cube, octahedron, dodecahedron, icosahedron—discovered by Pythagoras and popularized by the philosopher Plato.

polygon A planar region bounded by segments. The segments bounding the polygon are its sides, and their endpoints are its vertices.

polyhedron A solid bounded by polygons. The polygons bounding the polyhedron are its faces; the sides of the polygons are its edges; the vertices of the polygons are its vertices.

polynomial An algebraic expression that is the sum of the products of numbers and variables.

positive number Any number whose value is less than zero.

postulate See AXIOM.

prime number An integer greater than 1 that cannot be divided by any positive integer other than itself and 1. The first few prime numbers are 2, 3, 5, 7, 11, 13, 17, etc.

proof The logical reasoning that establishes the validity of a theorem from axioms and previously proved results.

proportion An equality of ratios of the form $a/b = c/d$.

pyramid A polyhedron formed by connecting a point, called the apex, to a polygonal base by triangular faces.

Pythagorean theorem The rule about right triangles that states: if a, b, and c are the lengths of the three sides of a triangle, then the triangle is a right triangle if and only if $a^2 + b^2 = c^2$.

Pythagorean triple Three positive integers, a, b, and c, that satisfy the equation $a^2 + b^2 = c^2$.

QED The abbreviation for the Latin phrase *Quod erat demonstrandum*, meaning "that which was to be proved," with which mathematicians typically end their proofs.

quadratic equation An equation of the form $ax^2 + bx + c = 0$.

quadratic formula The formula that gives the 0, 1, or 2 solutions to a quadratic equation as $x = \dfrac{-b \pm \sqrt{b^2 - 4ac}}{2a}$.

radius (1) The distance from the center of a circle to any point on its circumference. (2) A line segment of this length with one endpoint at the center of a circle and the other endpoint located on its circumference.

ratio The fraction obtained by dividing one number by another.

rational number A number that can be expressed as a ratio of two integers.

real number One of the set of numbers that includes zero, the positive and negative integers, the rationals, and the irrationals.

rectangular number A positive integer that can be written as $m \cdot n$ for some integers m and n both greater than 1.

regular polygon A two-dimensional polygon such as an equilateral triangle or a square in which all sides are congruent to one another and all angles are congruent to one another.

regular polyhedron See REGULAR SOLID.

regular solid A three-dimensional polyhedron in which all faces are congruent regular polygons and all vertices have the same degree. Pythagoras proved that there were only five such objects: tetrahedron, cube, octahedron, dodecahedron, icosahedron. Also known as PLATONIC SOLIDS or REGULAR POLYHEDRA.

right angle An angle with a measure of 90°.

right triangle A triangle with one right angle.

ruler-and-compass construction A plane geometrical diagram that can be created with the use of a ruler or straight edge to draw line segments and a compass to replicate distances and draw circular arcs.

Saccheri quadrilateral A four-sided plane figure used in the study of non-Euclidean geometries having two right angles adjacent to each other and two congruent sides opposite each other.

second A unit of angle measure equal to 1/60th of a minute.

semicircle Half of a circle.

sexagesimal Base-60.

sextant A mechanical device used to measure the angle between two distinct objects; used mainly in navigation to determine longitude.

similar triangles Triangles in which the corresponding angles are congruent and the corresponding sides are proportional in length.

simultaneous equations Two or more equations relating the same variables that are to be solved at the same time. Also known as a SYSTEM OF EQUATIONS.

sine For an acute angle in a right triangle, the ratio of the opposite side to the hypotenuse.

sphere The set of all points in three-dimensional space at a given distance, called the radius, from a fixed point, called the center.

spiral A planar curve traced out by a point rotating about a fixed point while simultaneously moving away from the fixed point.

square (1) A four-sided polygon with all sides congruent to one another and all angles congruent to one another. (2) To multiply a quantity times itself; raise to the second power.

square number A positive integer that can be written as n^2 for some integer n. Also known as a PERFECT SQUARE.

summer solstice The longest day of the year measured from sunrise to sunset.

system of equations See SIMULTANEOUS EQUATIONS.

tangent For an acute angle in a right triangle, the ratio of the opposite side to the adjacent side.

tetrahedron A regular solid having four congruent faces, each of which is an equilateral triangle. Also known as a TRIANGULAR PYRAMID.

theorem A mathematical property or rule.

triangle A polygon with three vertices and three edges.

triangular number A positive integer that can be written as $1 + 2 + 3 + \ldots + n$ for some integer n.

triangular pyramid See TETRAHEDRON.

trigonometry The study of right triangles and the relationships among the measurements of their angles and sides.

trisect To cut into three equal pieces, as a line segment, a geometric figure, or an angle.

unit fraction A fraction whose numerator is 1, such as 1/2, 1/5, or 1/139.

versed sine For angle θ, the versed sine is $1 - \cos(\theta)$.

vertex The endpoint of a segment in a geometric figure.

vertical angles Two nonadjacent angles formed at the intersection of two lines.

water screw Device invented by Archimedes of Syracuse consisting of a hollow tube coiled around a cylinder. Also known as an ARCHIMEDEAN SCREW.

FURTHER READING

Books

Anderson, Marlow, Victor Katz, and Robin Wilson, eds. *Sherlock Holmes in Babylon and Other Tales of Mathematical History.* Washington, D.C.: Mathematical Association of America, 2004. Collection of 44 articles on the history of mathematics through the 18th century.

Ashurst, F. Gareth. *Founders of Modern Mathematics.* London: Muller, 1982. Biographies of selected prominent mathematicians.

Bell, Eric T. *Men of Mathematics.* New York: Simon and Schuster, 1965. The classic history of European mathematics from 1600 to 1900 organized around the lives of 30 influential mathematicians.

Boyer, Carl, and Uta Merzbach. *A History of Mathematics.* 2nd ed. New York: Wiley, 1991. A history of mathematics organized by eras from prehistoric times through the mid-20th century; for more advanced audiences.

Eves, Howard. *Great Moments in Mathematics (before 1650).* Washington, D.C.: Mathematical Association of America, 1983. Presentation of 20 major mathematical discoveries that occurred before 1650 and the mathematicians involved.

———. *An Introduction to the History of Mathematics.* 3rd ed. New York: Holt, Rinehart and Winston, 1969. An undergraduate textbook covering the history of mathematical topics through elementary calculus: accessible to high school students.

Gillispie, Charles C., ed. *Dictionary of Scientific Biography.* 18 vols. New York: Scribner, 1970–1980. Multivolume encyclopedia presenting biographies of thousands of mathematicians and scientists; for adult audiences.

Grinstein, Louise S., and Paul J. Campbell, eds. *Women of Mathematics: A Biobibliographic Sourcebook.* New York: Greenwood Press, 1987. Biographical profiles of 43 women, each with an extensive list of references.

Heath, Sir Thomas L. *A History of Greek Mathematics.* 2 vols. New York: Dover, 1981. Detailed information about Greek mathematicians.

———. *The Thirteen Books of Euclid's "Elements."* 3 vols. New York: Dover, 1956. Translations with commentary of Euclid's book on algebra, number theory, and geometry.

Henderson, Harry. *Modern Mathematicians.* New York: Facts On File, 1996. Profiles of 13 mathematicians from the 19th and 20th centuries.

James, Ioan M. *Remarkable Mathematicians: From Euler to von Neumann.* Cambridge: Cambridge University Press, 2002. Profiles of 60 mathematicians from the 18th, 19th, and 20th centuries.

Katz, Victor J. *A History of Mathematics: An Introduction.* 2nd ed. Reading, Mass.: Addison Wesley Longmann, 1998. College textbook that explains accessible portions of mathematical works and provides brief biographical sketches.

Morrow, Charlene, and Teri Perl, eds. *Notable Women in Mathematics: A Biographical Dictionary.* Westport, Conn.: Greenwood Press, 1998. Short biographies of 59 women mathematicians, including many 20th century figures.

Muir, Jane. *Of Men and Numbers: The Story of the Great Mathematicians.* New York: Dover, 1996. Short profiles of mathematicians.

Newman, James R., ed. *The World of Mathematics.* 4 vols. New York: Simon and Schuster, 1956. Collection of essays about topics in mathematics, including the history of mathematics.

Osen, Lynn M. *Women in Mathematics.* Cambridge, Mass.: MIT Press, 1974. Biographies of eight women mathematicians through the early 20th century.

Perl, Teri. *Math Equals: Biographies of Women Mathematicians + Related Activities.* Menlo Park, Calif.: Addison-Wesley, 1978.

Biographies of 10 women mathematicians through the early 20th century, each accompanied by exercises related to their mathematical work.

Reimer, Luetta, and Wilbert Reimer. *Mathematicians Are People, Too: Stories from the Lives of Great Mathematicians.* Parsippany, N.J.: Seymour, 1990. Collection of stories about 15 mathematicians with historical facts and fictionalized dialogue; intended for elementary school students.

———. *Mathematicians Are People, Too: Stories from the Lives of Great Mathematicians.* Vol. 2. Parsippany, N.J.: Seymour, 1995. Collection of stories about 15 more mathematicians with historical facts and fictionalized dialogue; intended for elementary school students.

Reimer, Wilbert, and Luetta Reimer. *Historical Connections in Mathematics.* 2 vols. Fresno, Calif.: AIMS Educational Foundation, 1992–93. Each volume includes brief portraits of 10 mathematicians with worksheets related to their mathematical discoveries; for elementary school students.

Tabak, John. *The History of Mathematics.* 5 vols. New York: Facts On File, 2004. Important events and prominent individuals in the development of the major branches of mathematics; for grades 6 and up.

Tanton, James. *Encyclopedia of Mathematics.* New York: Facts On File, 2005. Articles and essays about events, ideas, and people in mathematics; for grades 9 and up.

Turnbull, Herbert W. *The Great Mathematicians.* New York: New York University Press, 1961. Profiles of six mathematicians, with more detail than most sources.

Young, Robyn V., ed. *Notable Mathematicians: From Ancient Times to the Present.* Detroit, Mich.: Gale, 1998. Short profiles of mathematicians.

Internet Resources

"Biographies of Women Mathematicians." Agnes Scott College. Available online. URL: http://www.agnesscott.edu/lriddle/women/women.htm. Accessed March 4, 2005. Biographies of more than 100 women mathematicians, prepared by students at Agnes Scott College, Decatur, Georgia.

"Eric Weisstein's World of Scientific Biography." Scienceworld. Available online. URL: http://scienceworld.wolfram.com/ biography. Accessed February 12, 2005. Brief profiles of more than 250 mathematicians and hundreds of other scientists. Links to related site Mathworld, an interactive mathematics encyclopedia providing access to numerous articles about historical topics and extensive discussions of mathematical terms and ideas, by Eric Weisstein of Wolfram Research.

"History of Mathematics." Simon Fraser University. Available online. URL: http//www.math.sfu.ca/histmath. Accessed January 19, 2005. A collection of short profiles of a dozen mathematicians, from Simon Fraser University, Burnaby, British Columbia, Canada.

"Images of Mathematicians on Postage Stamps." Jeff Miller. Available online. URL: http://jeff560.tripod.com. Accessed March 6, 2005. Images of hundreds of mathematicians and mathematical topics on international stamps, with links to Web ring of mathematical stamp collecting, by high school math teacher Jeff Miller.

"MacTutor History of Mathematics Archive." University of Saint Andrews. Available online. URL: http://www-groups.dcs.st-andrews.ac.uk/~history. Accessed March 5, 2005. Searchable, online index of mathematical history and biographies of more than 2,000 mathematicians, from the University of Saint Andrews, Scotland.

"Math Archives." University of Tennessee. Available online. URL: http://archives.math.utk.edu/topics/history.html. Accessed December 10, 2004. Ideas for teaching mathematics and links to Web sites about the history of mathematics and other mathematical topics, by the University of Tennessee, Knoxville.

"Math Forum." Drexel University. Available online. URL: http://www.mathforum.org. Accessed March 3, 2005. Site for mathematics and mathematics education; includes "Problem of the Week," "Ask Dr. Math," and *Historia-Matematica* discussion group, by School of Education at Drexel University, Philadelphia, Pennsylvania.

"Mathematicians of the African Diaspora." National Association of Mathematics. Available online. URL: http://www.math.buffalo .edu/mad. Accessed March 1, 2005. Includes profiles of 250 black mathematicians and historical information about mathematics in ancient Africa.

"Mathographies." Bellevue Community College. Available online. URL: http://scidiv.bcc.ctc.edu/Math/MathFolks.html. Accessed March 4, 2005. Brief biographies of 25 mathematicians, prepared by faculty members at Bellevue Community College, Bellevue, Washington.

"Wikipedia: The Free Encyclopedia: Mathematics." Available online. URL: http://en.wikipedia.org/wiki/Mathematics. Accessed August 22, 2005. Online biographies with many links to in-depth explanations of related mathematical topics.

ASSOCIATIONS

Association for Women in Mathematics (www.awm-math.org) 4114 Computer and Space Sciences Building, University of Maryland, College Park, MD 20742-2461. Telephone: 301-405-7892. Professional society for female mathematics professors; Web site includes link to biographies of women in mathematics.

Mathematical Association of America (www.maa.org) 1529 18th Street NW, Washington, D.C. 20036. Telephone: 202-387-5200. Professional society for college mathematics professors; Web site includes link to the association's History of Mathematics Special Interest Group (HOM SIGMAA).

National Association of Mathematicians (www.math.buffalo.edu/mad/NAM) Department of Mathematics, 244 Mathematics Building, University at Buffalo, Buffalo, NY 14260-2900. Professional society focusing on needs of underrepresented American minorities in mathematics.

National Council of Teachers of Mathematics (www.nctm.org) 1906 Association Drive, Reston, VA 20191-1502. Telephone: 703-620-9840. Professional society for mathematics teachers.

Index